"*Not Alone* is a rich, deeply textured book that seems to open like a blossom the further you get into it. First comes the fleshing out of an account featuring one of eleven widows from the Bible, enhanced by the author's imagination. Then a first-person account from the widow herself, almost as if Miriam Neff had interviewed her. These pieces are infused with empathy and the sensitivity only another widow could have painfully gained. And Miriam follows each treatment of these courageous women with a thoughtful Bible study. Not for widows only, this is a revealing dip into Scripture from a woman who has treasured it most of her life. Miriam's late husband Bob was one of the kindest and humblest men I ever knew. I couldn't help thinking how pleased he must be at how she has channeled her grief into such effective ministry."

—JERRY JENKINS, novelist and biographer,

JerryJenkins.com

"When you experience great and sudden loss—like the death of a spouse—suffocating feelings of isolation can close in all around. Friends and neighbors shrink back, unsure of what to say or do, and couples aren't certain how to include you in things. In a winsome and personal way, Miriam Neff helps the reader successfully navigate this difficult and complicated new world. It's why I happily give a double thumbs-up to her new book *Not Alone*!"

—JONI EARECKSON TADA, Joni and Friends

International Disability Center

"*Not Alone* is filled with unexpected surprises. Although you might think you are acquainted with these special women of the Bible, Miriam Neff lifts them out of their ancient context and transports them to our own day. We learn that trials can be expected but grace meets us in our disappointment, loneliness, and loss. Read it and share it with a friend!"

—DR. ERWIN and REBECCA LUTZER, The Moody Church

"Writing with the heart and experience of a widow, Miriam Neff has captured the struggles and heartache of widowhood as few others can do. Her insight into these eleven widows from the Bible will bring practical help and great comfort to those who have travelled this road, and give great insight to those of us who have many friends who are widows. This is a book of healing and hope for the often-overlooked widows in our world."

—MARY LOWMAN, director of women's ministries, The Moody Church, and founder of The Christian Working Woman radio ministry

NOT ALONE

Not Alone

11 inspiring stories
of courageous widows
from the Bible

Miriam Neff

REGNERY
FAITH

Cataloging-in-Publication data on file with the Library of Congress
ISBN 978-1-62157-633-4
e-book ISBN 978-1-62157-653-2

Published in the United States by
Regnery Faith
An imprint of Regnery Publishing
A Division of Salem Media Group
300 New Jersey Ave NW
Washington, DC 20001
www.RegneryFaith.com

Manufactured in the United States of America

10 9 8 7 6 5 4 3 2 1

Books are available in quantity for promotional or premium use. For information on discounts and terms, please visit our website: www. Regnery.com.

Distributed to the trade by
Perseus Distribution
www.perseusdistribution.com

To the many widows who have told me their stories.
Stories of murder and betrayal, as well as tender moments
and blessings. You have broadened my understanding
beyond my own experience. My compassion has grown.
I trust that will be true for each person who reads this.

Contents

Introduction

Walk with me on the dusty road from Moab to Bethlehem. I am young, athletic, and hungry for a new life. And smart enough to look away and not make eye contact with the rugged ruffians on the path. My name is Ruth.

Walk with me as two of the king's men escort me to an obscure entrance to his palace. My husband, my king's elite soldier, is on the front lines of the battlefield. This escort makes no sense. Curiosity in my soul is crowded out. Dread grips my mind and then wraps its tentacles around my heart. I am Bathsheba.

Weep with me as I hear of the murder of my friends' infant boys, all because King Herod wants my son dead. I feel as if a sword is piercing my soul! I remember a prophecy about my babe. Extreme joy mingled with terror. What next, Lord? My name is Mary.

Welcome, dear reader, to my world. Yes, these stories are fictionalized. Details added from my imagination, yet tethered to the truths in the Word. Each of these women gained my respect for characteristics we each wish for: courage, tenacity, generosity, compassion, competence. It just happens that they are all widows, as am I.

How did I start on this journey of first studying these women, admiring them, then teaching their stories, studying their context, and finally writing my fictionalized view of their lives?

It started in Ouagadougou, Burkina Faso. Several hundred young widows packed into an open-air church. My great desire as the speaker was for them to know how much God loved them and cared for them in their challenging circumstances. I taught from the stories of the widow of Zarephath and the widow and her pot of oil. These stories bridged the cultural divide of my life and theirs. Knowing I buried my husband, as had they, we shared the look of knowing, of mutual compassion.

I hungered to know more of the lives of these courageous women in the Word. So I studied, pored over maps, and imagined. I found myself disappearing into the lives of eleven women who lost their husbands. I entered their world, struggled to feel with them, understand what propelled them to be the kind of women they became. I wanted to be like them.

My desire for you, dear reader, is first that you enjoy the stories. Let these women earn your respect, then learn from them, as I have, that our circumstances do not define our destinations. Some today are referred to as adulterers, prostitutes, some unnamed and rarely held up as admirable women. I see them differently.

Their stories also reach into the lives of those not women or widows. Their examples, through extraordinary challenges, birthed boldness, industry, and courage in my own heart, and are in the most read book of all time.

ONE

GENEROUS
The Widow Who Gave Two Coins

Luke 21: 1-4

Tithes and offering time. Wealthy leaders loved this tradition. The large copper receptacle was moved front and center. Jewish leaders stood, shoulders back, and straightened their luxurious robes. Horns blared and the procession began. As each stepped up to the receptacle, he threw in large handfuls of valuable coins. Gifts from their wealth clanged loudly as many large coins rolled off the sides, making their noisy way to the bottom.

The most pompous, wishing to appear to be the most pious by the size of their gifts, maneuvered or manipulated their way to be first. Their coins resounded longer as they circled to the bottom of the receptacle. As coins filled the treasury, their resounding ring was shorter, landing on top of the filling copper receptacle, giving the giver fewer moments in the limelight.

One in particular bragged to his friends that his tithe was larger this time as his spice production was his greatest ever. He boasted of his most successful harvest of mint, dill, and cumin.

The other Pharisees applauded his success, though some secretly felt there was a discrepancy somewhere. The truth of the matter, known by some in the community, was that this Pharisee, who was honor-bound to care for his aged father and mother, was neglecting them. In fact they were often hungry and cold. Yet their pride-filled son was lauded for his public generosity.

The wealthy teachers of the law offered their tithes and turned to walk back to their positions. Barely veiled arrogance showed on each face. Proud of their perceived intellectual wisdom, savoring their status in the synagogue, they relished the looks of gratitude and sometimes envy of those whose gifts were small.

Hovering at the back of the gathering was a widow. Her shoulders drooped and her clothing was threadbare. Losing her husband too soon had ushered her into poverty. Gleaning what was left over in fields, she sent her children to carry wood for the wealthy, or sweep the shop floors of the prosperous tradesmen, and they brought home whatever they could. She slipped out quietly. She had no tithe to offer, not now, and probably not ever.

The more she was shunned for her poverty in the neighborhood, the more heavily she leaned on God. She knew from stories of widows in the past that God had helped them in their deep distress. And now, she prayed, fervently, frequently, and desperately.

Just when there was not one more drop of oil or handful of grain to make a cake for her children, a shopkeeper would give her son an extra few handfuls of grain to take home. Or her daughter would come upon a swath of unharvested grain at the remote edge of some field. Scooping up the left-behind grain, her daughter raced home thrilled to help prepare dinner. Food for another day.

And this widow, whose name we don't know, would gratefully thank God as she laid her tired head on her mat at night. "You know me. You see me. In my distress and disgrace, You alone have fed me and my children. I love you more today, Lord, than yesterday!"

And she would sleep, the deep sleep of peace, of acceptance of her new life.

⸻

I had not had the courage to go through my husband's things. A few worn robes—we never had wealth. A small bag with a few of his things, a carving knife his father gave him, I dared not open it, knowing a flood of tears would follow. Touching what he touched would be too painful.

Healing was slow. God became more precious. On the evening of my son's twelfth birthday, I sensed a stirring in my soul that it was time to move forward in some way in this new life I neither expected nor chose. I spent the late afternoon talking with my children about their father. My son had more questions than usual. He seemed older than his years, concerned about matters of a young man, not a boy. I wished to have a special meal like the kind we enjoyed on special occasions when my husband was alive. We had no lamb or even figs or dates. We ate our simple cakes and thanked God.

Lying down on my mat that night, I realized that while talking of my beloved husband was a time of laughter and many tears, I was not troubled, but comforted by the events of the day. Talking of his habits, his favorite phrases, even his mannerisms, was good. I sensed the same in my children. It was as if talking of their dad was healing, freeing, allowing them to move forward.

It was time. I approached the corner where I hid them and reached under the coverlet, almost reverently collecting my husband's tunic and the small bag he left. I wrapped myself in his tunic, almost imagining I could still breathe in his scent. I sat and allowed memories of him to flood over me like a gentle shower.

He farmed our small plot outside the walls, but that was not enough to sustain us. Others with more land hired him as a laborer. Times of planting, times of harvest, he rose before dawn and returned after dark exhausted, but content to know he was doing all he could. Rarely was he paid with money. I was grateful when he was given a lamb, grain, or oil. I was frugal. With the birth of our two children, they never lacked for enough to eat. Yet, they never had surplus. Just enough. Being given a lamb, it was tempting to slaughter it and enjoy meat. But we agreed to wait, to delay that satisfaction.

While I saw to the lamb's health and growth, my children saw this animal as their playmate. Killing it was difficult. But reality meant we needed food. God continued to provide. Looking back I thought those were the best days of my life. I took the ordinary for granted.

In spite of my heart's desire to replay those peaceful days, a scene forced itself against my will into my mind. My husband's lifeless body wrapped in the coarse fabric of a poor man's burial cloak. He had collapsed on the threshing floor of a wealthy landowner, immediately lifeless. His friends had gathered him into a cart and brought him quickly and directly to our small home.

Death was ever a part of life. I was not able to shield my children from that reality. They were clinging to me as the cart stopped at our door. Did his friends think he would suddenly rise and greet them? Did they think the familiarity of his home would shock him out of some strange trance? They carried him in and laid him on the floor. I hovered over him, cuddling his face in my hands. Even the touch of our children's hands on his did not awaken him. Speechless, they shared the communion of mingled tears. If not for my children, I would have been powerless to act. But for them, I would rather have joined my precious husband in death.

I had to act. Rising, I asked my neighbor to watch the children. I helped lift my lifeless husband into the cart, carefully covering his face with the rough wrap. I settled in, cradling his head in my lap. As the cart jostled to the edge of the city, I held his shoulders, gently protecting him from crunching motions. I caressed the strong muscles of the man, my husband, my lover who had provided for me, had given me children, loved, indeed cherished me. I bent over him moving the wrap ever so gently from his face as if to feel him take a gentle breath. I willed my body and mind never to forget those last caresses. No breath. I tucked the wrap around his face with finality and straightened. We rode together out to where he would be buried among the poor.

———

My chin bounced lightly on my chest, abruptly awakening me. Asleep, awake, no matter. I felt more comfort than pain reliving those memories. I wrapped his worn cloak more tightly around me and reached cautiously for the small bag he left.

Hesitantly I reached in, and began to examine the contents. I remembered the carving knife, a small whittled bowl, worn parchment with family names. Should I add our children's names to the parchment? Thinking the bag empty, I heard a small noise as I dropped it on my mat. I reached back in, deep in a corner, and there were a few small coins. I was astonished! Grateful! They were not worth much, but it was something. I sensed God's assurance more than I had ever experienced before; *I will take care of you.*

I fell asleep wrapped in my husband's tunic. I dreamed of our simple wedding, our days together, our nights together. I dreamed of our delight at the births of our children. I felt the warmth of his body next to me. I dreamed of all the significant days of my life past. The small bag lay next to me on the mat.

The next day nothing had changed. I put my husband's things tenderly back in the corner. Yet everything had changed.

In my poverty, I began to see those around me who were also poor. Overlooked, marginalized, I sensed compassion rising in my soul for those more desperate than I. In fact, one day as I was gleaning behind the harvesters in the field of a wealthy Pharisee, my daughter and I took note of an older woman bending slowly. With gnarled hands she gathered what she could. As we were about to leave the field at the same time, I approached her and asked if we could speak with her.

The old woman looked away in shame, but my offer to share our grain with her and even carry it to her home was an offer she could not refuse. We walked slowly together to a hovel not far from our own. Stepping inside to deliver the extra grain, we noted an old man lying on a mat. He turned his head to stare at us though watery eyes. Unlike our tiny home, this place was unkempt. Mats needed to be shaken in the sun. The odor caused our noses to burn.

The old woman quickly motioned us back out the door as if ashamed for any to see her and her husband in their present state. She grasped us, muttering thanks as tears rolled down and dripped off her chin. It was as if poverty had carved crevices in her aged cheeks through which tears of pain could flow.

Inquiring about their circumstance at the well the next day, I learned they were the parents of a wealthy Pharisee. He was known as a hardhearted man who took advantage of any and all he could, caring only for himself. At one time my emotions would have flamed at the injustice. No more. I experienced it, had come to expect it, and realized that the plight of the poor, lack of justice and no mercy, was a common bond. I shared that bond with many, including the old woman and old man.

I asked my son that night to pronounce the blessing on our bread. We bowed in humble appreciation. My daughter bubbled over in describing the events of our day. She was troubled, yet filled with compassion for the old woman and man. My son listened. A lively discussion followed. Troubled by the old couple's neglect, we knew we were powerless to change that proud son. Pharisees had great power. Better not to annoy them. We determined to do what we could.

―――

The next day the old woman was again gleaning near us. "May we come to your home again?" we asked. She tried to straighten her back and look into our faces. She would see only kindness there. My son met us at their door. We were welcomed in. My son, who knew of death from his father, gently lifted the old man and moved him to a different mat. We set about taking the mats, coverlets, and tunics outside and shook them. We swept the tiny floor and carried in a bit more water to wipe the forehead of the old man.

As my son gently lifted the old man and placed him on a fresh mat, a tear escaped the old man's eye. He turned his head to hide his pain from this young stranger. Quicker than he could turn, my son gently wiped his tears, patted his sunken chest, and asked God to bless him with peace.

Our little family rejoiced that night and felt the wealth of God's blessing hovering over our home.

Days passed. A realization came to me. God had provided us with so much. I would give those coins, the only ones we possessed, back. At the next offering time, I would go forward and give back to Him who was loving us through each hardship.

So I did. With a sense of urgency, I entered through the women's gate. A line was forming in the women's court near one of the temple receptacles. Wealthy Pharisees were again at the front. I took my place at the end of the line. A strange and comforting sensation flooded me, directing me to look toward a group of men standing back from the line. The eyes of one in particular caught my attention. He gazed at me intently, as if he could read my life. His gaze was comforting, full of compassion. Could this be the prophet spoken of at the well? Some believed him to be an impostor, others the promised Messiah. Rather than being invasive, his look of knowledge was affirming.

No one's look had ever penetrated my soul as his did. Not even my precious husband who knew me so well, trusted, and cared for me as best he could. Surely no one but the Messiah could see my life, understand my loss, and yet look at me as though I were worthy, capable, and precious.

I grasped the two coins. Gently rubbing one of them, I felt the imprint of the cornucopia, the horn of plenty with the pomegranate in the center. I knew I would never experience such lavish abundance on my table, nor ever even see such. But my contentment in that moment was overwhelming. Knowing God's goodness without abundance in any material way in my life was greater than I ever imagined I could experience.

Taking the other coin, my thumb moved slowly over the anchor. I knew that symbolized the fleet of ships one wealthy high priest had owned. I knew I would never even see the sea. No matter. My children were growing strong, healthy, and more importantly, compassionate. Great wealth indeed.

Turning the coin, I felt the eight-rayed star. I delighted in looking up at night and seeing the starlit beauty that could not be captured on a coin. The benefit of mere metal coins was fleeting. The wealth I possessed could neither be taken from me nor even measured.

The trumpet sounded. The time for receiving tithes began. I looked as one Pharisee strode proudly to the coffer. I heard his name mentioned, the son of our new precious elderly friends. He dropped in handful after handful of large heavy coins. They jangled loudly through the jar to the bottom proclaiming his great generosity. He turned to walk back to his friends. He was the one! The proud son impressed his peers with his generosity. He "gave" to God without using a bit of it to care for his aging parents.

As I awaited my turn, I gave all thoughts of the Pharisee to my Lord. My thoughts turned instead to new ways I could serve the poor around me.

It was my turn. One foot in front of the other; walking up to the treasury jar was something I had never done. Yes, I felt eyes on me. Whether it was pity for my worn shawl or their knowledge that I was a widow, it did not matter. I drew my shawl a bit more over my face. Simply standing in front of that receptacle, recognizing that my God would receive my tiny gift, inspired me to stand tall. I clutched the coins, pressed them to my lips whispering my husband's name, and thanking God, I released them gladly. Only two coins clanged their short way, a small noise to be sure. But I felt even more closely the presence of my much loved Lord. I turned and walked back, light of step, and full in heart.

Little did she know the very Son of God, the Son of the One to whom she prayed daily, was watching her.

And more, He called those He was training to Him, pointing to her. Throughout the centuries, though no one would know her name, she would become an example of generosity to millions.

Calling his disciples to him, Jesus said, "Truly I tell you, this poor widow has put more into the treasury than all the others."

STUDY GUIDE
LUKE 21: 1-4

Generosity. Do you ever feel that what you give is small compared to the resources others give? I certainly do. I'm tempted to shrink in generosity, believing I don't make a difference. Jesus says otherwise. One of his teachable moments with his followers occurred when, in Jewish tradition during worship, each person walked to the receptacle where tithes and offerings were deposited. Front and center, conspicuous, the offerings of all were watched and heard.

We don't know her name. Her shoulders may have been sagging and her clothing worn. But a widow gave all she had. And *she* became famous down through the ages for her generosity.

Her action, highlighted by Jesus, is worthy of following as an example.

> As Jesus looked up, he saw the rich putting their gifts into the temple treasury. He also saw a poor widow put in two very small copper coins. "Truly I tell you," he said, "this poor widow has put in more than all the others. All these people gave their gifts out of their wealth; but she out of her poverty put in all she had to live on" (Lk. 21: 1-4).

> Jesus sat down opposite the place where the offerings were put and watched the crowd putting their money into the temple treasury. Many rich people threw in large amounts. But a poor widow came and put in two very small copper coins, worth only a few cents.

> Calling his disciples to him, Jesus said, "Truly I tell you, this poor widow has put more into the treasury than all the others" (Mk. 12: 41-43).

STUDY QUESTIONS

1. Why did Jesus choose this widow as an example of generosity?
2. Besides money, what other resources did believers in the Old and New Testaments give to God?
3. What temptations do we who have little face?
4. What temptations do we who have much face?

THINKING IT OVER

The Bible says much about money. Here are a few examples.

Enjoy what you have with a grateful heart.

    Command those who are rich in this present world not to be arrogant nor to put their hope in wealth, which is so uncertain, but to put their hope in God, who richly provides us with everything for our enjoyment (I Tm. 6: 17).

Love God, not stuff.

    Keep your lives free from the love of money and be content with what you have, because God has said, "Never will I leave you; never will I forsake you" (Heb. 13: 5).

Provision begins in the family.

    Anyone who does not provide for their relatives, and especially for their own household, has denied the faith and is worse than an unbeliever (I Tm. 5:8).

Woe to you, teachers of the law and Pharisees, you hypocrites! You give a tenth of your spices—mint, dill and cumin. But you have neglected the more important matters of the law—justice, mercy and faithfulness. You should have practiced the latter, without neglecting the former (Mt. 23: 23).

It all belongs to God.

Honor the LORD with your wealth, with the first fruits of all your crops (Prov. 3: 9).

The earth is the Lord's, and all that is in it, the world and all who live in it (Ps. 24: 1).

Let no debt remain outstanding, except the continuing debt to love one another, for whoever loves others has fulfilled the law (Rom. 13: 8).

Establish your income and then determine how you will spend it.

Put your outdoor work in order and get your fields ready; after that, build your house (Prov. 24: 27).

PERSONAL APPLICATION

1. Recount some of the blessings you are enjoying today.

2. In what ways can you give back to God, or "pay it forward" helping someone else in need?

TWO

FOCUSED
The Widow at Zarephath

Part I—I Kings 17: 8-16

Her shoulders sagged as she bent and picked up sticks to make her final meal fire. Drought ravaged the land. She and her son would soon die of starvation. But not today. She had oil and flour for one more meal. People walked past her to the nearby water well. To them, she was invisible. After all, she was a widow. A few more sticks and she'd be on her way home. Out of sight of those who ignored her anyway. But she'd treasure this last meal with her son.

Keturah's mind replayed the turmoil of the past years that brought her to this place. She grew up here in Zarephath, a sleepy town on the sea. The coastal road brought travelers through it, but few stayed. Tyre, a maritime trading port and Sidon, a merchant destination, offered opportunity.

Her family's home was large enough to serve as an inn to travelers passing through. She learned the tasks of inn keeping: washing bedding, baking loaves to sell to their clients, purchasing oil at the market. Keturah was always curious. She loved to listen to the traveling tales their guests told at the evening meal time. As a teenaged girl, it would be inappropriate for her to sit with them as her father did. But she could listen as she served, observe their ways, and wish for a bigger life.

Between tasks she walked to the seaside, precious moments of solitude and dreaming. What could life be like if she lived in the city? She drank in the scent of the sea, felt its spray on her face, and longed for more in life.

Four merchants would be staying this evening, which meant today would be a day of washing bedding and shopping in the market for more produce. Each day seemed too much like the one before. But tonight's group would prove to be a bit different.

———

I brought fresh loaves to the table. As I listened to their conversations, there were apparently three generations here and a young merchant. It was hard not to gaze too long at him. My heart skipped a beat as he caught my glance and held my gaze as well.

Mollusks, wool, purple dye. I'd heard these topics before, but hearing this young merchant speak of them, they suddenly were much more interesting topics than before. Somehow I knew he had a curious mind also. Their conversation was lively. They were anticipating success in the markets at Tyre in the coming days.

Cleaning the table after they had gone to the upper rooms for the night, I hoped to see him again. His name was Laban.

I began to dream of what it would be like to be loved, to marry. While I knew that was my family's expectation, I had never really thought about it, until I saw Laban.

A few days later my father entered the kitchen at midday. His news must be unusual as he avoided our area of bustle, heat, and chatter as any man would. He motioned for my mother and me to join him in the courtyard.

"The merchants from Tyre will be here again tonight," he stated simply as a matter of fact, and then looked at me as if trying to discern my thoughts. "They would like you to join us, Keturah. Laban's cousin, uncle, and great uncle would like to make your acquaintance."

I felt out of place in my best tunic sitting at the table with the merchants. In fact, they asked little of me, but rather inquired of my father about my training. They seemed surprised I knew so much about Tyre and trading there. I was thankful for my curious mind and all I had learned as an innkeeper's daughter listening to the travelers passing through.

I was grateful my father taught me to keep the parchments of our inn's transactions. Laban took special note of that as well. The evening passed too quickly. I slept, willing myself to never forget the face of Laban, the most handsome young man I ever met.

The months following that evening were a blur. Shortly thereafter, Laban's family proposed our marriage to my father. I read his heart through his eyes. He would have preferred I marry someone in our village. What father wants to see his eldest move to a bustling city, foreign in so many ways, with dangers uncommon to Zarephath? But it would be a good life, a secure life. This merchant group was successful.

Our wedding proved to be quite the event for Zarephath. My father brought our inn to its finest hour. Repaired, polished, the courtyard brushed, and plants nurtured to appear their best for the occasion. My mother and her friends outdid themselves with platters of figs, dates, and wine as if they were expecting an army. Two lambs were butchered and there was no end to loaf baking.

Laban's relatives filled our inn and all other rooms in our tiny town. I hardly remember the ceremony. But I'll never forget my first night with Laban. I wanted nothing more in life than to bask in his love and give back to him as much pleasure as he gave me.

I took little with me to Tyre. My mother did insist on my taking an oil pot we used daily. I took it to the market countless times to buy oil. Carrying it home was a satisfying, short journey. Soon the oil mixed with ground wheat filled our home with the smell of fresh loaves baking. Yes, this familiar pot traveled with me to my new home.

Life in Tyre was exciting, more than I ever dreamed. Laban and I had small quarters in the commercial section, little more than a closet behind a trading area. With heads nearly touching over the small table in our cramped space, we pored together over the parchments of his fledgling business. Most of his time was spent working with his cousin in the family business. But I sensed his passion to be his own. Wealth did not drive him. Challenge, adventure, success in a new thing kept him dreaming, and us working as a team for hours while others slept.

Laban proved to be a successful merchant in his own right. While his relatives were a source of wisdom and introductions, Laban's instincts served him well. He became a successful mollusk trader. He acquainted himself with the seamen who went to the deeper areas where the more rare and valuable mollusks could be found. He learned what bait they used to suspend from their floats. He learned that the volume of mollusks needed meant partnerships among small groups, or investment in many boats.

I relished hearing the conversations in the shop, learned, and began to dream with Laban about what could be.

Exciting as this was, I did not always fully embrace city life. I missed those quiet days in our family inn when no guests demanded our efforts. I walked to the sea and remembered Zarephath. Back in our tiny home, I lifted the oil pot I still used and tried to remember the smell of fresh loaves at home. Here the smell of the mollusk trade made such comforting scents impossible. But I loved Laban and our dreams more than I longed for the comfort of the past. Industrious and hard working, I learned quickly what to look for when wool merchants came to our shop. They brought samples of the wool they wanted to dye. Wool from Damascus was most highly prized. I purchased a bit if a reasonable price could be reached. I knew I could use these to create valuable garments.

Our main business was to buy mollusks and create dye. Selling this precious dye was more profitable than trading in gold. We continued to buy fine wool with hopes for a new business as well. Possibilities for the future were endless.

Laban was known as a fair merchant. He was trusted.

With his profits Laban soon acquired his own boats for harvesting mollusks. Dispatching his own boats into the sea to the places where shells would produce the deepest purple became his specialty. But business was more than shelling in the most productive spots. The process of producing dye required intense oversight. The volume of shells required and the putrefying process of extracting dye from their glands required us to secure space outside the city. The boiling down process created a dye not only beautiful, but durable for decades. The small amount of dye extracted from thousands of mollusks meant scarcity. This translated to great cost and great profit. And where wealth is created, thieves were ever present to steal what was precious.

In time we had to move to a bigger commercial space. Merchants came because Laban was trusted by those who dyed wool. Those merchants supplied rulers and royalty, robes so valuable they were part of tribute gifts and inheritance. Tyre was *the* place to be. Bustling, alive with opportunity, city life consumed me, and into this life our son was born. We moved to the outskirts for space for our family. We enlarged our commercial area to accommodate a secure area for our prized dye and more space to entertain merchants.

I loved to walk to the seaside beach where our boats were tied. The breeze from the water swept all concerns aside in those moments. What would the next mollusk harvest bring? How many would produce deep purple? What price would dyes of a lighter shade bring? Is our shop secure? On occasion there were robberies, even attacks on successful merchant shops.

The breeze whipped up and sent spray into my face. Looking out to sea, the free feeling of my younger years pushed all concerns aside and replaced the uncertainty of my current life. All questions disappeared for the moment like mist on the breeze. We had a healthy, curious son. Already, at age eight he was learning the trade. He was allowed to go out on the boat of our most trusted mollusk harvester, Nahor. Life was good.

So much to do. In two days our most consistent traders would come to purchase dye. Laban's labor and skill would be rewarded and we would plan the next season. Days at the inn prepared me well. I baked extra loaves for the merchants, organized flasks of wine, prepared trays of figs. Hospitality was the center of all discussions.

I stirred from my bed, a sense of foreboding enveloped my soul. Laban was not at my side. He had stayed late at our shop. The most valuable dye had just been processed. In the darkness I slipped on my robe and quietly went to our common area, careful to not awaken our son. No Laban.

It would be unthinkable to leave our home during the night. My only option was to wait for daylight. I huddled under the bed covers, my mind racing. Our shop was in a better area of the city, but robberies did occur there. The faces of our workers circled through my mind. Sometimes wealthy people were held for ransom, even their children. I tiptoed to my son's pallet. He turned slightly, drew a deep breath, and slid his hand over his tousled hair. Surely all would be well.

Dawn came before sleep. I leapt at the sound of a knock at our door and flung it open. Laban's foreman stood with a look of despair, staring at me. "Come," was all he could utter.

Grabbing my shawl and clinging to his arm, I hurried through the streets toward the merchant center. The quiet of the streets did not soften the wild drumming of my heart. I sensed a presence surrounding me unlike any I'd ever experienced. It was strangely soft, surreal, yet close and tender. "You are a widow now," the presence communicated. Frozen, I jerked Nahor to an abrupt halt. "Impossible," I thought. We rushed on. The presence prevailed. "You are a widow now. Have no fear. I'll not leave you alone."

The merchant scene was surreal. The door was ajar, not destroyed. I stepped in, rushing to bend over Laban's slumped body, stepping in the blood pooled around him on the floor. I knew before my eyes could confirm the fact. My Laban was dead.

Keturah lay over her beloved's body breathing into his hair, drinking in the scent of his familiar body she had loved for so long, willing him to suddenly take a deep breath and return to her. It did not happen.

"Laban, Laban," Nahor sobbed. He knelt beside us, laid his worn hands on both of us. And then a howl of anguish filled the room. It was Nahor's voice, but my heart's cry.

Nahor moved to the smashed-in door of the inner area where the valuable dyes were kept.

He peered into the storage area for the purple dye. The room was empty.

The blur of the following days brought moments of numbness to Keturah. But she would not allow herself to succumb to grief.

Their son needed her strength to get through this. There was the wrapping of Laban's body in spices, the burial, hours of wailing outside their front door. There was small comfort in the expected traditions. Bringing food, expressing shared grief—Keturah had done these acts for others. Surely this was not real. The violence of Laban's death brought nightmares. Old age or illness could be accepted. This crime, his murder, defied understanding, defied acceptance.

I began to see that my friends and even business merchants looked at me differently.

I saw in the questioning eyes that followed me, all wondering why, how, and who? I wondered too. No answers were forthcoming. Rumors flew. Was one of his trusted workers turned to betray him? Nahor secured our boats. Why go to sea when there is uncertainty of what to do with the catch? Laban's merchant friends offered to buy the tools of our business. Their offers were small. My anger grew as I realized they cared nothing for my future or that of my son, but only the opportunity to greedily grasp what Laban had built for themselves.

I tried to sort out what to do with the chaos of our business. Oversee it myself? I knew much. But would our workers respond to my oversight?

I would seek wisdom at the seaside. Approaching our boats, I saw Nahor cleaning them. As I came to him, he glanced up with a questioning look of surprise. I would seek his counsel. After all, he was Laban's trusted laborer from the early days. His words did not bring comfort. He had been offered other work. I could not assure him of our future.

My dreams for our son to partner with his father were shattered, like Laban's body on the cold floor of his death. Could all the workers be trusted? Laban opened the door to someone. And then he was murdered, his treasured dyes stolen. Laban would not have opened the door to a stranger.

Weeks passed. I stumbled to the seaside again seeking the refreshment it always brought me. The sea was shrouded in mist. Were my eyes playing tricks on me? Where were our boats? The wind whipped up bringing no refreshment but rather pelting spray. I knelt on the shore, pressed my forehead in the sand, and sobbed until my exhausted body could not make another sound.

A soft sense of strength from within brought me to lift my head. The mist was gone. A sure sense of direction formed in my mind. It was time to move home.

Keturah and Hadad unloaded their few belongings into the home of her childhood. With what little she could salvage of their business interests, she could live here in the familiar. She might even open the old doors as an inn again. The boats were sold without her knowledge. At least they were sold, not stolen. Her elderly parents had moved in with her brother. At least Laban's cousin helped her sell what she could and secure ownership to this place. This was not the life she had dreamed of, but it was what she had. And she had Hadad. It seemed he

looked more like his father every day. And he was curious.
They had each other.

———

Famine was gripping the land. Before she could build a
secure future here, harsh heat and no water left livestock dead.
Once-green fields were turning brown. There was little to do
now but try to survive until rain came again. As parched as her
tiny lot was, her soul was more so. Were it not for precious
Hadad she would welcome death.

The sounds around her shook Keturah to the present. A bony
sheep bleating, resisting being dragged down the street. Voices of
women on their way to the well. Familiar sounds. Yet today it all
sounded so foreign. She needed to focus on one of her last tasks.
Gather sticks to make the last meal for Hadad and herself. Starvation loomed. She could welcome death, but not for her son.

"Would you bring me a little water in a jar so I may have a
drink?" A male voice speaking to her. A rare occurrence. A
request she could honor, it would cost her nothing. Tucking the
few sticks she had gathered into her tunic, she went toward the
well careful to stay out of the way of the others.

"And bring me, please, a piece of bread."

Her Gentile heart, no doubt, tightened. She recognized he
was a Jew, not of her people. Recognition compelled her to
answer. She had some knowledge of the God of the Jews. Was
her heart cynical? Curious? Or just afraid?

"As surely as the Lord your God lives," she replied, "I don't
have any bread—only a handful of flour in a jar and a little olive

oil in a jug. I am gathering a few sticks to take home and make a meal for myself and my son, that we may eat it—and die."

This man, Elijah, spoke with calm and kindness. Her weary heart lifted a bit as she took in his next request.

"Don't be afraid. Go home and do as you have said. But first make a small loaf of bread for me from what you have and bring it to me, and then make something for yourself and your son. For this is what the Lord, the God of Israel, says: 'The jar of flour will not be used up and the jug of oil will not run dry until the day the Lord sends rain on the land.'"

———

I hurried home with a heart full of conflict. Do I share the bit I have which means my son and I die sooner?

He is a Jew; I'm a Gentile. Would he ask this same sacrifice of a Jewish widow? Can I trust him?

I've heard of his God, some good and some bad. What if he is right and it's my miracle in this drought? The only hope of my son's survival?

My son and I will both die anyway, sooner if this man is not a man of truth.

I chose to do as he asked. What risk was I taking? He was just a thirsty, hungry man. But this God of Israel, I'd heard, had more than great powers. He had compassion for people in hard places.

Lifting the oil jug I used in my childhood, I poured a bit on a mound of flour. Kneading it I pondered. His God? Was such a miracle even possible for a Gentile? Word had spread of this man and his influence. What was rumor? What was true?

I slapped the ball of dough on the heated interior of my tiny jar oven. Watching it carefully, I pealed it off and hurried back to find the unusual man.

His manner surprised me. Rarely did Jewish men speak to Gentile women. If they did, rarely did they speak with respect and kindness. He took the loaf, thanked me, and I hurried home, my heart racing. I uttered words that surprised even me. "God of Israel, if you are who some say you are, now is a really good time to show up!"

Hadad was waiting at the door, a rapt look of excitement on his face. "The jar! It's filling!" I rushed and bent with him over our jar. More oil. Indeed, he was a holy man.

His word was true! Flour appeared for the next meal. Miracle of miracles!

I hurried back to find the man of God. Still at the gate, I approached humbly and invited him to return to our inn. Surely if he provided life for Hadad and me, I could spare the upper room of the inn for his comfort.

Our oil pot never emptied. Nor did our jar of flour. Each day they filled, and the next, and the next—until rains came again.

Time passed. We resumed our lives. On our small plot of land we grew grain again. The olive tree in our courtyard produced in abundance. I began to buy wool again, weaving it to sell garments. I could not yet afford the rich purple dye I once used. But I was resourceful. Hadad had the merchant heart of his father. I knew the day would come when he would leave Zarephath and our inn. For now, we were busy with travelers on their way between Tyre and Sidon.

As Hadad and I served them, I noted not just his interest in their conversation, but his joining them; ideas grew, as did friendships. I no longer listened. That life was behind me now. This simple life was all I needed.

I noticed a change in my neighbors. They no longer looked at me with disdain, a poor widow. They nodded approval when I sold olive oil at the market. Those with daughters looked over-long at my son. The scars of tragedy became the birth of inde-pendence and resolve.

It is suggested that Elijah perhaps lived in Keturah's home for two years. We know she and her son survived because she stayed focused. We also know the seed was planted for this Gentile widow to know the one true God. The God who Elijah repre-sented. But she did not fully embrace Him, yet. One day at a time, one task at a time, one meal at a time. A good example for us all.

STUDY GUIDE
I KINGS 17: 8-16

Staying focused on the task at hand sometimes feels impos-sible in crisis situations. Anxiety and out-of-control circum-stances threaten to immobilize us. Consider the widow of Zarephath. She was gathering sticks to cook a last meal for herself and her son: a handful of flour, a little oil, with starvation looming.

While she was gathering, the prophet Elijah asked her to give him a drink. Easy. Water was available. The next "ask" was to first make food for him and then her family! Hard stuff. Yet she focused on who Elijah represented, and acted. One loaf for the prophet and then one for her. Yes, there it was! Oil in the pot and flour for one more loaf. Would this be her last? Stay in the moment. Focus. She did. And the oil and flour lasted until prosperous days came again.

"Go at once to Zarephath in the region of Sidon and stay there. I have directed a widow there to supply you with food." So he went to Zarephath. When he came to the town gate, a widow was there gathering sticks. He called to her and asked, "Would you bring me a little water in a jar so I may have a drink?" As she was going to get it, he called, "And bring me, please, a piece of bread." "As surely as the Lord your God lives," she replied, "I don't have any bread—only a handful of flour in a jar and a little olive oil in a jug. I am gathering a few sticks to take home and make a meal for myself and my son, that we may eat it—and die."

Elijah said to her, "Don't be afraid. Go home and do as you have said. But first make a small loaf of bread for me from what you have and bring it to me, and then make something for yourself and your son. For this is what the Lord, the God of Israel, says: 'The jar of flour will not be used up and the jug of oil will not run dry until the day the Lord sends rain on the land." She went away and did as Elijah had told her. So there was food every day for Elijah and for the woman and her family. For the jar of flour was not used up and the jug of oil did not run dry, in keeping with the word of the Lord spoken by Elijah (I Kings 17: 9-16).

STUDY QUESTIONS

1. What emotions might the widow at Zarephath have felt in her first meeting with Elijah?
2. Why might this widow have been tempted to not trust Elijah?
3. What emotions have you experienced during times of stress and loss?

THINKING IT OVER

Let's look at what God's Word says about emotions.

He walks with us on our journey whether we sense His presence or not.

The Lord is with me; I will not be afraid. What can mere mortals do to me? (Ps. 118: 6)

He offers us a new day in which the necessity of making different choices becomes the opportunity to change.

The Lord has done it this very day; let us rejoice today and be glad (Ps. 118: 24).

The Lord upholds all who fall and lifts up all who are bowed down.

The eyes of all look to you,
and you give them their food at the proper time.
You open your hand
and satisfy the desires of every living thing.
The Lord is righteous in all his ways
and faithful in all he does.
The Lord is near to all who call on him,
to all who call on him in truth.
He fulfills the desires of those who fear him;
he hears their cry and saves them (Ps. 145: 14-19).

Yes, we fall in the crisis, but we do not stay down. Our Lord takes our hand when we are down, and lifts us up. While Scripture does not tell us this widow's feelings, surely this situation evoked strong emotions.

Facts we know about emotions:

Our emotions are intense with the death of a spouse. Why? Two became one and now half of us is ripped away. Every aspect of our life changes, like it or not, ready or not.

Our emotions must be acknowledged. Denial is not a healthy permanent option. We need much wisdom to act biblically when our emotions are strong.

Our emotions can become empowering and energizing and a positive force as we create a new life. I realize this may be hard to believe if you are in those early months or years.

PERSONAL APPLICATION

1. What step of faith might you consider in using what little you have to bless another? While others seldom lack food, it

might be encouragement or some other way you can bless another.

2. Consider that the widow's act of obedience and generosity would have been observed by her neighbors. Food through the famine. Ask God to give you strength and wisdom so others can see His love in your life.

PART 2: INDEPENDENT
I KINGS 17: 17-24

Death's grim reaper came knocking, again.

Zarephath is my home. My inn has been the temporary home of this man of God, Elijah. Who can doubt he is truly a man of God? Even my neighbors have seen his power. He proved it. Miraculous flour and oil in my kitchen through days of famine were his doing.

Why he stays here, I do not know. We are not his people. But I would be a fool not to allow him my upper room as his place. Hadad and I would have died of starvation if not for him.

And then, my son was becoming listless. Each morning I hoped to see improvement. Instead he was becoming more pale, his breath short and soft. His appetite waned. My neighbors could offer no wisdom. His illness was different. I stayed close, listening more intently every day to detect any improvement. I could hardly hear him breathing. I moved his pallet to our common room so I could be near him. Looking at his limp body hardly moving, I tried to remember the times in Tyre when we skipped to the beach. He delighted in running in the wind. His energy was boundless, like Laban's.

In the hours I sat by my son, my mind continued its backward journey to the good days in Tyre.

We named him Hadad meaning "sharp" just knowing his mind would be like that of Laban and I. He proved his name. After our jaunts to the sea, going back to our merchant shop, he never tired of pouring out his adventures to his dad. His quick mind matched Laban's. What would life have been had Laban not been murdered? Hadad did not grieve openly. I think he wanted to show me he could be the man his dad would have wanted him to be.

He proved to be so resilient. Leaving city life. Becoming son of an innkeeper in lazy Zarephath. Living in our plain home. Gone was the excitement of his dad's thriving merchant business. Gone was heading out to sea, pulling up the traps of mollusks. Gone was the site where the acrid smell of crushed mollusks signaled the harvesting of the precious dye from the glands of these sea creatures. Standing proudly by his father in our shop. Listening as Laban negotiated with those who bought dye. Negotiating to buy the best wool. Seeing his father expand to sell both dye and prized wool to merchants who specialized in making such fine robes they were considered trading items like gold, silver, and copper.

My reverie was interrupted by the unthinkable. Even the soft noise of shallow breaths was quiet. Hadad stopped breathing. I watched in disbelief. Surely he would shudder slightly like he did before and breathe again. His chest did not move. His face became gray. I wrapped him in my arms tightly pulling him to my chest, willing my breath to become his.

Anger, ever consuming me facing down death. I screamed!

Elijah hurried down the stairs. In my anguish, I lashed out.

"What do you have against me, man of God? Did you come to remind me of my sin and kill my son?"

My mind raced back to the days when I, as a resident under the king of Sidon, believed Chemosh was the greatest power on earth. I bowed to him, brought sacrifices, and believed, even in Chemosh's cruelty, that he would determine my fate. This god would choose the man I would marry, the children I would bear—I even offered sacrifice to him in order to ensure the success of our harvests. Ever thankful, I did not offer Hadad to him, my heart still burning with the memory of kneeling under the horrid statue of Chemosh as women threw their babes into his fiery belly. I had stayed on my knees!

The bitter taste of bile filled my mouth. Would this God of Israel, the one Elijah revered, now require that I pay up?

"Give me your son," Elijah replied. He took him from my arms, carried him to the upper room where he was staying, and laid him on his bed. I wished to charge up the stairs after them and cling to Hadad. My husband—gone. But my son—I could not bear it! Yet, Hadad was in the arms of Elijah. I sensed in my heart a comforting presence. "Both of you were carried in Elijah's arms. Have you forgotten the famine?" I sunk to my knees and waited.

———

Crying out to God was no new thing for Elijah. Seeing God's personal miracles was common in Elijah's life. Providing a cave with water during the drought. Sending ravens with bread and meat to feed him. Elijah knew with every fiber of his body that his God was great, powerful, and ever ready to answer any who called on Him in sincerity.

But even obedient prophets did not always know how, when, and even why God would act.

He cried out to the Lord, "Lord my God, have you brought tragedy even on this widow I am staying with, by causing her son to die?"

He laid Hadad gently on his bed and stretched himself out on the boy three times and cried out to the Lord, "Lord my God, let this boy's life return to him!"

God answered. His breath returned. Hadad could have run down those stairs to his mother. But Elijah carried him. Hadad clung to his neck as if they were one soul, not two. "Look, your son is alive!"

My anger changed to exuberance. "Now I know you are a man of God and the word of the Lord from your mouth is the truth."

Elijah placed him gently in front of me. I rose and hugged him tightly. I was overwhelmed seeing my son alive, feeling his warm cheek, hearing his breathing. Rising on my toes, as he had grown so, I gently kissed his forehead.

To some this would be a normal, if intimate greeting. But I had held his lifeless body. I was beholding, experiencing, a miracle. I felt a distantly familiar presence permeate my mind and heart, the same sense I felt rushing with Nahor to our merchant center. I could not have known of Laban's murder. Yet this Presence knew and cared enough for me to assure me of His care at the same time, revealing to me I was now a widow. Laban's murder, our protection, returning home, oil and flour throughout the famine. This Presence was the one true God. Elijah was more than a man of God. He was a man sent by the ONE true God. He came to me, rescued me, and had surely forgiven me or I would not be holding my living son.

I would embrace Him forever, repeat His miracles in my life until I had no breath. I might still be a Gentile by birth, but I would forever be a follower of the one true God. The God of the Jews.

The miracle of flour and oil caught the attention of the widow of Zarephath. But her heart's conviction came after seeing that Elijah's God had power over death.

STUDY GUIDE

Community is important. But sometimes we need to be independent—do something different like the widow of Zarephath. She was a Gentile of Sidon, yet she housed a male prophet, a Jew, for an extended period of time. His miracle, multiplying her flour and oil, saved her life, and her son's. Yet later her son died. She challenged Elijah. "Did you save him to now kill him because of my sin?" She would have been a worshipper of Chemosh, sensual and sinful indeed if she had participated in their rituals of worship. Scripture does not tell us her specific sin. Yet she recognized her life had not been what Elijah's God should honor.

Elijah brought her son back to life. Her response: "Now I know that you are a man of God and that the word of the Lord from your mouth is the truth." It took more than preventing death for her to believe. It took raising her son after he died for her to personally embrace God. Uniquely independent, this widow's willingness to ask for the impossible resulted in her salvation.

> Some time later the son of the woman who owned the house became ill. He grew worse and worse, and finally stopped breathing. She said to Elijah, "What do you have against me, man of God? Did you come to remind me of my sin and kill my son?" "Give me your son," Elijah replied. He took him from her arms, carried him to the upper room where he was staying, and laid him on his bed. Then he cried out to the Lord, "Lord my God, have you brought tragedy even on this widow I am staying with, by causing her son to die?" Then he stretched himself out on the boy three times and cried out to the Lord, "Lord my God, let this boy's life return to him!"
>
> The Lord heard Elijah's cry, and the boy's life returned to him, and he lived. Elijah picked up the child and carried him down from the room into the house. He gave him to his mother and said, "Look, your son is alive!"
>
> Then the woman said to Elijah, "Now I know that you are a man of God and that the word of the Lord from your mouth is the truth"(I Kings 17: 17-24).

STUDY QUESTIONS

1. Have you seen God help you through one challenge, only to question Him again when a new challenge emerges?
2. What steps can you take to remember God's help to you in the past?
3. What was the final evidence for this widow to believe the word of God is truth?
4. What evidence has God shown you in your life that He is truth?

PERSONAL APPLICATION

1. What provisions do you need today?
2. On whom are you depending to supply your needs?
3. Prayerfully consider your list. Which are needs and which are wants?
4. Recognize that God may provide what you need in unique and unexpected ways.

THREE

PERSISTENCE
The Widow and the Unjust Judge

Luke 18: 1-8

S he arrived at the city gate at the time the judge was to appear to hear the cases in his area. Her face was taut, lean, and lined. She had been thrown off the land she and her husband owned—by her own relatives! During her husband's illness, she assumed their attentiveness to her, her home and land, meant they would care for her after her husband's death. Wrong! They were assessing what they would soon take from her. The grain she helped plant—that her children could help harvest—would soon be harvested by those who had not toiled for it. They would not share precious barley with her and her hungry children.

Her only recourse was to go before the judge, state her case, and plead for justice. She remembered hearing Deuteronomy read to her people. Judges were to be fair. God is impartial and defends the fatherless and widowed.

Day after day she addressed him. He pulled his shoulders up to their most erect, smoothed his fine robe, turned, and walked away to be addressed by others. Others who could reward him for listening to their cases. Others who would ensure a prime animal for his dining, or an object of value, who would arrive at his doorstep after he ruled in their favor.

Day after day she returned to the shelter of a kind neighbor, Naarah, who agreed to temporarily take in her and her children. She knew this was temporary. Naarah's husband was kind. But kindness cannot feed three extra mouths. Surely the judge would hear her case.

Discouragement and bewilderment grew in her grieving heart. This judge's reputation was well known. He did not honor God's laws. His decisions were dictated by a heart that craved bribes and the accolades of people who would laud and bolster his importance. He cared nothing about having a reputation for justice. Who was God to decide matters? This was his domain. He cared solely about himself.

Each day her heart stirred as she saw her children shunned by their cousins. They knew, even in their young minds, that cousins playing in their courtyard was not right. Seeing the smaller loaves at their neighbors' table each night, they ate less. The look in their eyes was more than hunger. Hopelessness was creeping in.

———

Why go back? He has ignored me day after day. I cry out to him, "Grant me justice against my adversary." I realize mine is only one of many voices. But ultimately he must acknowledge me, hear my case. He points to another—again. I wait. I listen as others recount their injustices. This one has kept a person as servant after the debt was repaid. That person has been using false weights in his market place. Another has moved a boundary line in secrecy. Please, God, let me be patient. Their needs are important too.

The judge indicates he is done for the day. Wearily I return to my neighbors thinking, "Why bother?" Grief has depleted my strength. Being invisible at the gate in the presence of the judge is humiliating.

I enter Naarah's home. My children look expectantly. I shake my head. They look down, then go to the courtyard. They no longer venture out in the street to meet the friends they once played with and chased, carefree and happy, secure in the care of their mom and dad.

If I were alone, I would never return to that place for justice. But for them, I will.

So I went back. Again, and again. I was discovering within myself a strength I did not know I possessed. A sense of both fairness and fear battled in my soul.

Fairness won, persistence followed. I would not give up.

I went again to the gate. The judge would not even face me today. Still I cried out. No doubt he hoped I would be discouraged. No way! I followed even closer behind him. Those he addressed to hear their cases would see my face directly behind him today. My face. Though I was ignored and unheard, I would not be unseen. Though feeling invisible, I prayed. I knew God not only saw me, but heard me.

I sensed again today the judge's heart had not softened. He did not seek advice from those around him who could have confronted him in his arrogance. He never did. He simply became annoyed at my pestering.

At high noon, there was no one standing to state his case. He turned to leave for his midday nourishment and rest. He could not help but meet my gaze. His eyes were icy, stone cold, unfeeling as he looked down on my worn shawl, my gaunt face. It was as if I could read his mind. "I need not the approval of the weak god these people revere. I deserve this position as judge. My intellect, my thoughts, are so superior to theirs. But I'm tired of her. Her eyes look into mine like she might attack me if I don't hear her case. I'd make sure that would be her undoing. But enough. I'll hear her case and be done with her."

I looked resolutely into his stone-like gaze.

Did this pride-filled judge know enough history to remember God's words in Isaiah? Even I knew these teachings.

"Do not be afraid; you will not be put to shame. Do not fear disgrace; you will not be humiliated. You will forget the shame of your youth and remember no more the reproach of your widowhood. For your Maker is your husband—the Lord Almighty is his name—the Holy One of Israel is your Redeemer; he is called the God of all the earth" (Is. 54: 4-5).

I had a new husband, the Lord Almighty himself! The Holy One was my Redeemer. Being God of all the earth, He would be my protector!

The judge lifted his arm, indicating I could plead my case. A few hurrying past paused, then more collected. Everyone who passed by this gate daily knew I was here persistently. They also knew the judge never acknowledged me. Most even knew I was a widow who was thrown off my land. They expected me to give up, join the destitute of the city, and indenture my children so they would not starve.

But the judge lifted his arm in my direction. There was a sense in the air that something unusual was about to happen. I did not notice them. I had rehearsed my case so often that I laid out my case, hardly taking a breath.

"The land my husband and I possessed was passed down from son to son. You are well aware of the laws of the land, that land is the possession of the family. Given the death of my husband, my son is now the inheritor, the owner of this land. My brothers-in-law have thrown us out of our home, taken our land, and even now are planning to harvest the grain our family planted."

I paused. Though perspiration was running down my body, my mind was cool, focused. I spoke with strength and clarity.

"Declare who is the rightful owner of our land!"

A hush fell over the small cluster of listeners. All expected the judge to declare the brothers-in-law the owners. Then he would return to his home, probably to find a gift at his door. A choice lamb, a flask of fine wine. His reputation for greed was well known.

The judge made a startling declaration. "The land rightly belongs to you. Return today." There were collective whispers through the onlookers. Turning, he made his way through the small gathering, diverting his eyes from them.

———

As the judge entered his home, the aroma of freshly baked loaves greeted him. A servant girl laid cheese on the table and filled his glass. While others would have offered thanks for God's provision, he did not.

A strange knot formed in his stomach as he reached to put cheese on his warm bread. An unpleasant odor destroyed his appetite. He looked around. Nothing had changed in his familiar surroundings. The loaf was his favorite. He lifted his goblet. Yes, it was his favored wine from the vineyards of Galilee. He heard again the widow's voice repeating, pleading day after day for justice. He turned his goblet slowly and took a sip. The taste was acrid.

Abruptly leaving the table, he left to rest through the heat of the day. But rest did not come. He pondered the teachings from his early training. This God his people followed warned about taking advantage of His vulnerable people. There was something in the countenance of the widow that haunted him.

"Am I truly above God's reckoning?" The question burrowed into his mind before sleep and was his first thought when he awoke.

I left the village public area with a lightness of step I had not felt since before my husband's death. Straightening my shoulders, determination welled in my soul. Whatever testing lay ahead, I was ready. Repossessing my home would be anything but easy. Physical labor, continued marginalization in the community, disdain, even hatred from my relatives, these would not shake my new resolve. My greatest concern was how to convey the judge's message to my brothers-in-law. While my mind cried, "Lord, help me!" my heart reassured me He'd be there.

It seemed those few watching me had a different gaze, surprise tinged with a bit of respect. I realized news of the judge's pronouncement would travel quickly to my displacers. "Thank you, Lord."

Full of gratitude, I rushed into my neighbor's home. "Naarah," I cried. "I'll have my home back, my land!" She hugged me tightly. I drew my children to me filled with hope, wondering how to take the next step. I knew one thing without a shadow of a doubt. God *did* see me. God *did* hear me. He would not abandon me now. We bowed over our small meal and gave thanks.

My children and I lay down to rest through the hot hours. They fell asleep with the simple faith of children. Fully awake, I felt energized. Moving my lips in silent prayer, I thanked God again and again. I could not wait to return home. Later I planned with Naarah and her husband. We would go to my home in the morning together.

I realized that with the loss of so many friends and even relatives I once trusted, the few friends I had now were more precious than ever. Many who I thought cared for me before did not have my best interests at heart. I could accept that; I had no choice.

Before daylight I was awake. I reassembled the few things I was able to take from my home that fateful day after my husband's death. I tried not to remember the harsh words they hurled at me. "You are responsible!" They screamed words of accusation and labeled me using wicked words I never wanted my children to hear. I covered my daughter's ears and hugged her to me as we ran and stumbled before them down the street. My son looked over his shoulder in disbelief. I willed myself to force those memories from my mind.

Today I would simply return home. We would start over together. We three.

My friends and I approached our home. The courtyard gate was ajar, one set of hinges missing. There was no stool under the olive tree, the trellis was smashed, and the grapevines cut to the ground. I prepared myself for the worst. Stepping into our common room, I saw that it was empty. Our furniture had been simple and sparse. I drew my son and daughter tightly and felt again the strong assurance I sensed before the judge.

"All will be well," I assured them. I believed that with every fiber of my body.

The days that followed were filled with hard work, delight to be back home, and the temptation to be bitter. We went together to our plot of ground. I feared the near full-grown barley would be gone, as well as our grapevines in the courtyard. We hugged each other in delight. Our barley was still standing! I pledged in my heart to share our harvest with Naarah's family. It was as if God increased our bounty during that harvest time.

We needed little in our home. I felt blessed with our new-found comfort in owning very little. With mats to sleep on, in time we might acquire a stool or two. But that was not a necessity. Having each other and our home was contentment enough.

I determined to not allow bitterness any room in my soul. Arriving at the well one day, I heard the name of the judge mentioned. And then seeing me, all of the women fell silent. They looked at me expectantly.

"I need no news of him. He stands before God. I have no room for bitterness or ill wishes. God knows. His care for me is enough."

Our family never returned to the status we had before. But my faith in God was beyond what I had before. And that, after all, is what's most important.

STUDY GUIDE
LUKE 18: 1-8

Becoming a widow typically means desolation, grief, loneliness, even bitterness and vulnerability. This is true today, and in biblical times. God our Creator recognizes human nature. While others may want to marginalize, even take advantage of vulnerable people, God says, care for them.

He created laws for His people clearly stating widows were to have access to the legal system for their grievances to be heard and addressed. This instruction was not always followed. Jesus, ever tender-hearted toward the marginalized and vulnerable, told a parable to his disciples for their instruction.

The widow in Luke 18 is an example worthy of our study. God's instructions are that widows are to be given justice. They are vulnerable and God says not to mess with them. The judge, however, ignored her and would not hear her case. Had someone moved her boundary, taken her land, enslaved her children? We don't know. Financially greedy folks today do attempt to take advantage of widows. I know that from experience.

This widow just kept showing up! And the unjust judge kept ignoring her. He admitted he neither feared God nor cared what people thought.

Finally, he listened because he was annoyed.

Persistence, my friend. For a just cause, don't give up.

Then Jesus told his disciples a parable to show them that they should always pray and not give up. He said: "In a certain town there was a judge who neither feared God nor cared what people thought. And there was a widow in that town who kept coming to him with the plea, 'Grant me justice against my adversary.'

"For some time he refused. But finally he said to himself, 'Even though I don't fear God or care what people think, yet because this widow keeps bothering me, I will see that she gets justice, so that she won't eventually come and attack me!'

And the Lord said, "Listen to what the unjust judge says. And will not God bring about justice for his chosen ones, who cry out to him day and night? Will he keep putting them off? I tell you, he will see that they get justice, and quickly. However, when the Son of Man comes, will he find faith on the earth?" (Lk. 18: 1-18)

STUDY QUESTIONS

1. Why are widows seen as vulnerable?
2. Have you experienced people attempting to take advantage of you as a widow?
3. You may find this applicable and helpful whether you're a widow or not. If so, what helped you be strong?

Identify trusted people you can reach out to for support and counsel when you are exploited.

God's Word is clear that widows should not be exploited:

For the Lord your God is God of gods and Lord of lords, the great God, mighty and awesome, who shows no partiality and accepts no bribes. He defends the cause of the fatherless and the widow, and loves the foreigner residing among you, giving them food and clothing (Dt. 10: 17-18).

Appoint judges and officials for each of your tribes in every town the Lord your God is giving you, and they shall judge the people fairly. Do not pervert justice or show partiality. Do not accept a bribe, for a bribe blinds the eyes of the wise and twists the words of the innocent. Follow justice and justice alone, so that you may live and possess the land the Lord your God is giving you (Dt. 16: 18-20).

The Lord tears down the house of the proud, but he sets the widow's boundary stones in place (Prov. 15: 25).

God's Word is equally clear that He can help you be bold:

Do not be afraid; you will not be put to shame.

Do not fear disgrace; you will not be humiliated.
You will forget the shame of your youth
and remember no more the reproach of your widowhood
For your Maker is your husband—
the Lord Almighty is his name—
the Holy One of Israel is your Redeemer;
he is called the God of all the earth (Is. 54: 4-5).

We spoke earlier of emotions. This widow, no doubt approached the judge with misgivings and doubts. Imagine her elation to finally get justice! Persistence means one must often hear many "no" answers before hearing "yes."

As we said earlier, our emotions can become empowering and energizing and a positive force as we create a new life. I realize this may be hard to believe if you are in those early months or even years of loss. Remember this widow's example.

PERSONAL APPLICATION

1. Pray for God's wisdom and intervention in each matter in your life, no matter how small or great.

2. Communicate with other godly "counselors" to encourage you and even appear with you when opportunists attempt to take advantage of you.

3. Pray for God to bless you with persistence to pursue justice in any area of your need.

FOUR

FAITH-FILLED
The Widow and
Her Pot of Oil

II Kings 4: 1-7

She was a respected wife. Obadiah, her husband, was a prophet. Just, fair, and compassionate. King Ahab placed him in charge of the palace. He recognized his business and leadership ability and trusted him. Moreover, he knew the people respected Obadiah. While many hated both Ahab and his wife Jezebel, Obadiah served his king fairly. Better to keep a man like Obadiah close to him. Obadiah chose not to live in the palace, but rather to have his own home nearby with his wife and two sons.

She stood erect in the community. She diligently mothered their two sons. Since the crowning of Ahab as king of Israel, she and Obadiah had watched with great distress as he built a house for Baal, even erecting an altar for worship to this terrible, foreign god. They believed in the God of Israel as the only true God who would not share supremacy with any other. They knew God would not be silent for long. Indeed, the prophet Elijah predicted a drought in the land.

51

Heat came hard. Dry winds whipped dust through the fields not ready for harvest. Crops withered and lay without heads of grain. Streams dried and the beds became hardened. Empty veins ran through them rather than water.

———

These hard times came at the hands of Queen Jezebel. A murderous woman, she was killing off the Lord's prophets. Day after day my husband heard the orders of this wicked woman. He could neither contradict her nor openly defy her. Yet his convictions could not be ignored. My Obadiah took action. He took one hundred prophets and hid them in two caves. He committed to supplying them with food and water, a decision I supported. What would become of us if no prophets were left alive to receive instruction and guidance from our one true God? Our home became a collecting place for grain. My friends and I prepared loaves. Our sons delivered food and water taking different routes to the caves. They watched carefully and varied their delivery times so as not to attract attention from Jezebel's followers. Packing our sons bags with loaves for the prophets, I prayed.

"Lord, hide them from our enemies. Keep them sure footed climbing through the wilderness. Bring them safely home. Amen."

I noted our sons were changing. Once playful and light-hearted, that blissful stage of freedom from care gave way to being more serious. Their cave visits created a vigilance, an awareness of a world they were protected from before. They were learning that their father's faith was uncommon. Others in our neighborhood entered the house of Baal. My sons sensed the profound faith of their father, evidenced through his actions. Only great faith would merit such great risk.

The hidden prophets welcomed our sons into the caves, wanting to know news of their communities. They praised Obadiah for his conviction, his provision, and prayed for protection for all who continued to believe.

My sons' safe return brought relief to my soul and energized me. I rose another day to oversee the grain being brought in, baked, and packed yet another delivery to the caves.

While Obadiah paid for early deliveries of grain, I noticed a change. Obadiah was no longer paying, but accepting a parchment indicating a debt to be paid at a later date. I was concerned, but pushed that unease aside. Obadiah had a sure position in the palace. His skill would ensure our income after this terrible season. Surely this would be a temporary thing. Jezebel could not be tolerated forever. God would remove her somehow, some way. Obadiah would repay the debt he was taking on personally. It would take time. But all knew his word was good, his reputation sound.

In time, Jezebel tired of her deadly search for prophets. Our hidden friends were able to return to their villages. Most were silent, fearing for their lives. Life serving in Ahab's palace began to take a greater toll on my husband. He no longer had courage to counteract the evil of the palace edicts. He became listless. I thought that the season would pass. His faith would renew his spirit.

One morning I awakened to touch his body. It was cold and stiff. I recoiled in disbelief and touched him again. Surely he would breathe ever so lightly, then more deeply. No breath. My Obadiah was dead. King Ahab and Queen Jezebel sent the customary condolences. I listened as a woman of stone. I believed his service to them brought his death. This was not due to his sin, but due to the profound demands on him watching their wicked ways and being at their service.

Our family went through the ritual practices of mourning. I was numb and hardly remember our friend's generous gifts of food and kind words. I only remember the sounds of wailing in my ears. Even louder was the pounding of my heart in the night hours. How could we go on? What would become of our sons?

Obadiah left us with few resources. I presumed we would uncover more as I made my way through each day and began to look for what provisions he would surely have left us.

Trips to the market before my widowhood were social times of pleasure and connection. I noted a change, an unwelcome one. Others began to avoid us and seemed to not wish to trade with us. They were treating me as though I was poor, no longer the wife of a respected prophet, but a widow with two hungry sons. I carried my pot to the one who sold oil and secured enough for one meal. We returned home to find a man at our door. I recognized him as one who sold grain to Obadiah earlier for the hidden prophets. Before he spoke he examined my sons carefully.

I could hardly believe the words he uttered. He came to claim them as slaves, to work for him paying off their father's debt. I was distraught. Burying my husband was beyond belief. My heart was shredded. To think of my sons as slaves was more than I could bear. I would have given my own life for their freedom, but a middle-aged woman was not a valuable slave. Two healthy boys were. I felt hopelessness wrapping me like a heavy, cold, wet cloak.

I pleaded with him to return in one week. I would pay all. I would find a way. He agreed, but I could see reluctance. He turned and walked away with confidence. Surely he was already planning the slave tasks he'd assign to my sons.

Elisha. I remembered this revered prophet. Surely he would help me. He would understand fully Obadiah's zeal to hide and feed the prophets.

I wanted to approach him respectfully, but my emotions were too raw. I cried out to him for help, pouring out my hopeless situation.

His response was puzzling. He asked, "How can I help you? What's in your home?"

"Only a small jar of oil." My heart was in turmoil. What difference would a small jar of oil make? But this was Elisha, a prophet I respected.

His instructions were puzzling. He asked me to borrow from my neighbors any pots they could spare. Would they loan their pots to me, this poor widow? Perhaps some questioned in their hearts if their pots would be returned. I had no option but to act.

Perhaps it was pity that prevailed with my neighbors. My sons brought many pots, many, many pots.

———————

Elisha could have miraculously filled all the pots himself. But his goal was to expand their faith, the faith of both the widow and her two sons, not his reputation.

He asked her, with her sons, to go behind closed doors and pour from her pot into each pot. Imagine their disbelief as oil kept flowing. Pot after pot until each was full. No doubt her tears mingled with the oil.

On Elisha's instruction, she and her sons sold the oil, which was enough to repay their debt and more to spare.

What happened behind that closed door was simply a miracle. We saw it! We touched it! My sons and I could never be challenged on the mighty and unlikely way God provided. We began the task of carrying each pot to market and selling its contents. With accuracy and careful accounting, I repaid the creditor until the debt was paid. This took days, joyful days. After each sale, we returned the pot to its owner. Each received it listening with astonishment to what happened with her pot!

God's heart for me and my sons touched each neighbor who had loaned a pot. They knew of the miracle.

As each woman daily picked up her pot, she no doubt thought, *A miracle happened right here in this piece of clay in my hand. God did a miracle! This empty pot became a source of food, of freedom, for my poor neighbor.*

When all debts were paid, we still had oil to use and sell. I went to the market with my sons standing tall. We were no longer shunned. Sellers welcomed us to look at their produce. Women greeted us. My sons played and roamed freely. A widow still, yet faith filled the void my husband left. I no longer felt my identity was the widow of a prophet. I was a much-loved daughter of God.

STUDY GUIDE
II KINGS 4: 1-7

The widow of a prophet, possibly Obadiah, was left with debts, which meant her two sons would be taken as slaves to pay them off. She cried out for help to Elisha, a prophet who knew her husband. He asked her to do a strange thing—borrow lots of her neighbors' pots, hibernate with her sons behind closed doors, and fill all the pots from the small jar of oil she had left.

Why follow such a strange directive? Because she was a faith-filled widow. While her husband let her down by not providing for her and leaving her in debt, she believed God would provide.

So many pots were filled and the oil sold that her sons remained free and they lived on the profit.

Imagine the impact on each woman who had loaned her a pot.

No doubt they, too, were inspired by her faith.

The wife of a man from the company of the prophets cried out to Elisha, "Your servant my husband is dead, and you know that he revered the Lord. But now his creditor is coming to take my two boys as his slaves."

Elisha replied to her, "How can I help you? Tell me, what do you have in your house?"

"Your servant has nothing there at all," she said, "except a small jar of olive oil."

Elisha said, "Go around and ask all your neighbors for empty jars. Don't ask for just a few.

"Then go inside and shut the door behind you and your sons. Pour oil into all the jars, and as each is filled, put it to one side."

She left him and shut the door behind her and her sons. They brought the jars to her and she kept pouring. When all the jars were full, she said to her son, "Bring me another one."

But he replied, "There is not a jar left." Then the oil stopped flowing.

She went and told the man of God, and he said, "Go, sell the oil and pay your debts. You and your sons can live on what is left" (II Kings 4: 1-7).

STUDY QUESTIONS

1. Where was this widow told to look first for a solution to her problem?
2. Are you experiencing a need now? First take inventory of what you have. How might God use what you now possess?
3. Besides this widow and her sons, who else observed this miracle?
4. What possible impact might this event have had on the community?

THINKING IT OVER

God delights in our planning; however, He may provide unseen solutions.

———

In their hearts humans plan their course, but the Lord establishes their steps (Prov. 16: 9).

———

Many are the plans in a person's heart, but it is the Lord's purpose that prevails (Prov. 19:21).

———

Your path led through the sea, your way through the mighty waters, though your footprints were not seen (Ps. 77: 19).

Obedience to God is often difficult because we don't see His outcome. However, God always rewards obedience. Obedience sends a message to God that your faith is in Him no matter what.

The one who calls you is faithful, and he will do it (I Thes. 5: 24).

———

With this in mind, we constantly pray for you, that our God may make you worthy of his calling, and that by his power he may bring to fruition your every desire for goodness and your every deed prompted by faith. We pray this so that the name of our Lord Jesus may be glorified in you, and you in him, according to the grace of our God and the Lord Jesus Christ (II Thes. 1: 11-12).

PERSONAL APPLICATION

1. Prayerfully make a list of your needs.
2. Consider carefully with whom you might share that list, asking him or her to pray with you and help you see possible solutions.

3. Write what initial action you might take to begin
   to discover a solution.

FIVE

EXPERIENCED
Naomi

The Book of Ruth

Impossible! How could it be, Almighty, that you have now taken my sons! Was it not enough that we were starving in Bethlehem and came to this godforsaken place simply because rain provided food in Moab? And you took my husband. Losing him created a hole in my heart, my life, my hope for the future. Too soon, Almighty! Too soon!

But my two sons. They would be my providers, my protectors. Yes, we named them Mahlon (meaning sickly, because he was a scrawny newborn) and Kilion (meaning failing, he struggled to breathe), but they grew to manhood. And, Almighty, I doubted that when they were infants.

———

The walk to Moab was tedious. Elimelek and I could have made the trip in five days. Mahlon and Kilion needed to go at their own pace. The heat was brutal. Leaving Bethlehem, saying goodbyes was hard. Some disagreed with our decision. We knew from past famines that the death toll was relentless. Elimelek was determined; I more so. I knew my frail sons were more vulnerable than most to hunger. Already thin, I feared for their lives.

Walking through the wilderness southward was depressing. I took no comfort in the familiar. We had walked through the dry heat of wilderness before. We knew our destination and knew we would eventually return home. I wished for some inner sense of assurance. None came. I pulled my sons' wrap further over their heads to protect them from the brutal sun and blowing dust.

Had we made the right decision? I questioned even more when we reached the cliffs nearing the Dead Sea. The descent was steep. We literally tied our family together with chords. Carefully, we edged and inched our way downward, pausing when we felt we could safely rest a bit. My legs burned. Was it exertion, fatigue, or fear?

We had gone too far to go back.

En Gedi was a welcome relief beyond my imagination. Water, date palms. We drank deeply and enjoyed a bit of variety from our dried fruit and the pita loaves we brought from home. En Gedi was not yet suffering from the drought. Had the heat affected my mind? I felt we had paused in a bit of heaven. We rested a whole day there. My sons delighted in exploring, even running. Too soon it was time to move on.

The walk to Masada was again barren and dry. After only twelve miles, again we slowed. Mahlon simply had no energy to hurry and Kilion found breathing more difficult. The blowing dust did not help. I urged him to try to keep his cloak over his nose and mouth. But what small boy follows his mother's instruction for more than a few minutes?

The barren landscape reminded me of why we were leaving Bethlehem. Yet I remembered our bed back home. How different from the hard ground we would sleep on tonight. I remembered comfortable, familiar neighborhood conversations on the way to the well. I felt tears coming, but swallowed them hard. My children needed to see me strong, not nostalgic. They did not even realize yet they would not see their friends for a long, long time. We pressed on. Why this nagging sense of fingers clutching my soul and tightening their grasp? Following my men, I took comfort looking at Elimelek's strong shoulders. One son on either side, each held one of his father's hands. Elimelek, my husband, my protector. All would be well.

I was thankful for the raisins we brought from home and our refilled water skins from En Gedi. I wondered what adventure the Dead Sea would bring. We would cross where a tongue of land juts out into the water. We heard higher water meant we would need to find a way to float across. Thankfully the water was low. We could wade through. Again, our chords were our security for little boys who might want to splash and attempt other antics in the water. Curiously, the water actually burned where I had been scratched climbing. Yet it was refreshingly wet. Elimelek explained the water was high in minerals including salt. Of course, our sons had to cup their hands and take a swallow. Scrunched faces showed they now knew why it was called the Dead Sea.

Stepping out on dry land again, I was struck with a poignant revelation. I was no longer in my homeland. God's promises did not apply here. His protection was not assured, His name not revered. I was not enveloped with a sense of foreboding, yet not of comfort either. I was now "Other." Not with my people. Would God still be my God here? Surely He would. He was Who He was, never changing. I would cling to that.

We found water springs soon and were thankful to refill our skins. It was another hard day's walk. My husband and sons slept soundly. My sleep was fitful, full of distorted images of Bethlehem and the cloud-covered terrain that lay ahead.

Finally, the last day of our journey. It was a steep climb up from the Dead Sea, but we were energized, knowing our destination was near. We arrived at the higher plateau of Moab approaching the city of Kir. This would be our new home.

Adjusting to Moab was not easy! Their culture of hospitality meant we were welcomed, fed, and offered safe sleeping quarters. My husband had been a carpenter in Bethlehem. He was welcomed for his skill. We were provided, or rather loaned, a small home. Food was abundant. Able to feed our growing sons, I could adjust to whatever life demanded. I was very aware I was "Other," but survival was more important than acceptance. I observed and learned their ways.

Strange food, strange habits, and worshipping Baal—how can they sacrifice their young, take innocent life? Almighty, You are known for giving life, preserving life. Yet, they did not drive us out. We are not starving here. Surely all will be well.

And my sons were now learning Elimelek's trade. We moved to a larger space of our own.

Evening. It was almost time for my men to return home. Freshly baked pita loaves were ready, goat cheese, grapes, and figs. What a feast compared to our homeland. My heart was light.

What was the commotion in our courtyard? I flung open the door to see my sons carrying Elimelek. My concern changed to horror as I saw Elimelek's face. There was no hint of color, no healthy brush of the sun on his checks. He was ashen gray. They laid him on a pallet. Holding him, I knew the truth could not be denied—Elimelek was dead.

We had no choice but to bury him in this strange land. I felt the weight of being "Other," without the gathering of familiar relatives and mourners. Our neighbors did not accompany us to the place where we laid his body. I would have succumbed to total despair. But I still had my sons.

A glimmer of hope prevailed. Even as a distraught widow, I trusted that my sons would marry. There would be children. My empty arms would cradle grandchildren. A new generation, new possibilities, that was the expected rhythm of life.

Mahlon and Kilion worked diligently at the business their dad started. What they lacked in physical strength, they compensated with their innovative minds and the foundation of their dad's teaching. Young Moabite women noticed them. While they were slight of body, ordinary in appearance, they were polite and showed kindness unlike Moabite men. Young women found that intriguing. Moabite fathers took note of their successful business. While not as vigorous as Elimelek, they were skilled at their trade.

In time Mahlon and Kilion were approached with offers of marriage. Arrangements were made. Orpah and Ruth? Not my choice; pagans for sure. But here we are. What choice did they have? Young men, with normal desires. I would adjust for the joy of a child's laughter, hope for the next generation. I would adjust.

While a household of five should be ordinary, I did not find it so. Ruth and Orpah cooked with strange spices, were content with coarse grinding of grains for bread. I found the strange scents almost sickening. They were kind to me, deferred to me. I never had to carry water. My sons were observant, remembering the scents from our mealtimes before. I thought I was covering my longing. I obviously failed. They purchased the parcel next door, erected a separate small home there. I had my own courtyard. With gardening room, I attempted to grow the familiar plants of my homeland. Yes, sometimes I was lonely beyond words.

Now ten years have passed and no grandchildren. I did not detect that Ruth or Orpah were unhappy, but their families could not help but be disappointed. While Moabites and my people were quite different, our cultures shared one trait. Sons were important and land ownership was tied to male heirs.

I noted Mahlon was becoming quite thin and Kilion's breathing was shallow. They struggled on together. I believed the high plateau meant the air might not be right in some way. I shared my concern with no one. After all, not only was this home to my daughters-in-law, my sons remembered little of Bethlehem. This was their home now.

I can hardly remember now how their deaths came about. There were rumors of an illness sweeping through Kir. Word was the gods were angry. I cared nothing for these baseless beliefs, until I heard it was only fatal for those already weak. That bit of news brought terror to my soul. In reality that illness did not touch them. But it awakened in me the recognition that their lives were fragile.

It was as if a blur and a covering of numbness blocked all remembrance. I welcome the numbness still, and prefer to have no memory of them in their wasted state. God has protected me from grief beyond what I could bear.

And now Mahlon and Kilion are gone. I buried them both.

Impossible, too much, too soon. And now this. I have buried my sons. I am utterly depleted.

I must return home. I hear there is food again and the land prospers. God has not blessed us here. Did He intentionally curse me for leaving our homeland? I will only know when my feet are on the soil where I belong. I packed with my daughters-in-law watching. In their way, they cared for me. They began to pack as well. What could I say? Somehow they believed their future was tied to mine.

I could only shuffle with a profound sense of despondency, choosing what few things we could carry for the trip back. News that the famine was over did not lift my spirits. Maybe we would find favor with my relatives, if they remembered I still existed. I continued to wonder why my daughters-in-law were willing to go with me. How would they be received? Moab was always the enemy of Judah, my people. They had ever been a well-remembered thorn in the side of God's true followers.

Somehow, they see strength in me, and I have come to love them. After all, they loved my sons. They were tender in my widowhood, consoled their husbands as Mahlon and Kilion would think back with wistful sadness on the loss of their dad. While comforting me, they listened as I spoke of you, Almighty. They listened.

And now they insist on coming back to my home. Risky travel and an unknown welcome. They cannot know how hard the journey back will be. I still remember. They may be pagans, but they are bold, and they do care for me.

———

They had not traveled far on the several-day journey when Naomi sensed this would not go well. She pleaded with them to go back.

"Orpah, Ruth, listen to me. Your parents will accept you back. You are young. You can marry again. Those are your people. My people are different."

Her look told both young women she feared for their acceptance in her tight community. But they refused, pledging their commitment to her regardless of the future. She pleaded, she begged, and her last argument, she felt, would convince them.

———

"Even my Almighty, whom I have clung to through all this, has turned against me. Surely you see that. How can I protect and provide for you when my protector and provider has abandoned me!"

Orpah was convinced. She turned and took those first steps back toward home. But Ruth clung to me. She refused to leave me. "Look at Orpah! She will soon be back in the familiar home of her mother. Friends, family, maybe even a new marriage to one of your people." Yet Ruth pleaded with me with words of commitment I can never forget.

"Don't urge me to leave you or to turn back from you. Where you go I will go, and where you stay I will stay. Your people will be my people and your God my God. Where you die I will die, and there I will be buried. May the Lord deal with me, be it ever so severely, if even death separates you and me" (Ruth 1:16-17).

Ruth clung to me. Her face of resolve was evidence that nothing would change her mind. We faced my homeland together and began walking toward the Dead Sea.

The road home was harder than before. Grief and age dogged my steps. Fear for Ruth began to consume me. Roadways and paths sometimes were the territory of thieves and ne'er-do-wells whose methods were violence. Selfish interests, lust, and greed ruled. We did not sleep near the paths. We found any crevice that would hide us from sight. I never felt those fears while traveling with my beloved Elimelek.

There were no women on our paths. We kept our eyes down when men passed us. They stared at Ruth. Wrapping ourselves tightly in our tunics at night, as we lay on the hard earth, I pleaded with the Almighty for safety. Surely in some corner of my soul, I knew my Almighty could not forsake me. I pleaded for Him to wrap Ruth in the same cloak of protection as He did me. I would no longer be "Other" in Bethlehem. But what was ahead for Ruth? Alien women were often assumed to be prostitutes. Poverty sometimes forced them to become that, against their desires. Could I protect Ruth? Surely not. Only the Almighty could. I remembered Ruth's words.

"Your people will be my people and your God my God."

"May the *Lord* deal with me."

"She has claimed You as her Lord. And you are God of your word! You have heard her vow, You will keep Yours. I give the burden I carry of protecting her to you. I cannot bear it. You, my Lord and God, certainly can." I slept soundly, at last.

Crossing the Dead Sea was uneventful, thankfully. Again, we could wade through the shallow water. My mind was flooded with visions of my husband and me holding tightly to our sons' small hands, splashing through the salt-laden water. Tears watered the smile I could not withhold. I would never forget.

Ruth noticed my tears and touched my cheek to brush them away. I learned through hardships that tears should not be denied or hidden. Let them do their cleansing work and communicate compassion. Share with onlookers the reality of life lived fully, the hardships and the blessings. Transparency so often births stronger love.

The trip from Masada to En Gedi was uneventful as well. En Gedi was more welcome than ever, more lush than I remembered. God was watering our land again. I knelt and gave thanks. We rested for a day. Though eager for home, I knew our arrival would not mean ease. Poor and disconnected, there would be challenges enough for me for tomorrow. Today we would rest.

Ruth and I filled our flasks for the steep climb. We gathered a handful of dates, a welcome addition to our depleted and stale loaf provision. The thought of Bethlehem invigorated me. Ruth thoughtfully tied my sash around her waist and forged ahead with strength and a spring in her step. In my eyes she was more than strong and beautiful. She had become a true daughter to me.

Home. Bethlehem. Slightly familiar faces stared at us.

Is that you, Naomi?

"Not really," I answered. "Call me Mara—bitter. I left full and now I'm empty. Almighty has dealt harshly with me."

How common for a widow's thinking to be skewed. Naomi left her homeland empty and hungry with her husband and two children who weren't the healthiest. She was returning with only a tenacious daughter-in-law who was not only fully committed to Naomi's well-being, but also embraced her Lord. In her grief, having lost her husband and two sons, Naomi could not see her blessings.

Naomi's people had customs to care for the widows and poor among them. They could go into the harvest fields behind the harvesters and glean what was left behind. Naomi knew the custom, the fields, and her relatives. She took action and directed Ruth to glean in her relatives' fields. Did Ruth feel fear at being behind the harvesters, avoiding their looks and maybe even their comments? After all, she was a disrespected, pagan widow. But she trusted Naomi, following each instruction.

The focus of Naomi's future was no longer Naomi. It became Ruth, the young woman she had urged to go back to Moab. This young woman who loved Naomi too much to abandon her, had come not only to respect, but also to love and embrace God, Naomi's only God, as her own.

Naomi, who thought meaning in her life was over, was wrong. A new chapter opened. Naomi had a future she could never have imagined.

Boaz, a near kinsman, followed the customs and laws, a process that allowed him to take Ruth as his wife. Yes, a son was born and Naomi experienced the joy of being a grandmother. The focus of this story is no longer Naomi, but Ruth.

The Book of Ruth is indeed a love story. But the focus is not the love of a man and a woman. It is the love story of Ruth for her new love: God the Almighty.

Ruth's statement of commitment to Naomi has been echoed through the centuries. It has been repeated because it says it all, in marriages, family commitments, and profound friendships. Ruth's vow is perhaps the most repeated of all vows, one of the treasures of the Book of Ruth.

STUDY GUIDE
THE BOOK OF RUTH

Experience is a valuable characteristic. The widow, Naomi, had that in abundance. She moved with her husband and two sons to a hostile country to escape famine. Her husband died. She experienced becoming a mother-in-law to two women her sons should not have married. Then her sons died. How could she provide for these two young women?

Her only thought was to retreat with them to her homeland. She called herself bitter. Her perspective was skewed by her grief. She thought God brought her misfortune. Yet, one daughter-in-law chose to follow God because of Naomi's example. Naomi, a real woman living in hard circumstances, set an example in such a way that Ruth wanted what she had! Read the Book of Ruth. The result was that Naomi's grandson was in the lineage of Jesus. Experience, real living—that's value.

> In the days when the judges ruled, there was a famine
> in the land. So a man from Bethlehem in Judah,
> together with his wife and two sons, went to live for a

while in the country of Moab. The man's name was Elimelek, his wife's name was Naomi, and the names of his two sons were Mahlon and Kilion. They were Ephrathites from Bethlehem, Judah. And they went to Moab and lived there.

Now Elimelek, Naomi's husband, died, and she was left with her two sons. They married Moabite women, one named Orpah and the other Ruth. After they had lived there about ten years, both Mahlon and Kilion also died, and Naomi was left without her two sons and her husband.

When Naomi heard in Moab that the Lord had come to the aid of his people by providing food for them, she and her daughters-in-law prepared to return home from there. With her two daughters-in-law she left the place where she had been living and set out on the road that would take them back to the land of Judah.

Then Naomi said to her two daughters-in-law, "Go back, each of you, to your mother's home. May the Lord show you kindness, as you have shown kindness to your dead husbands and to me. May the Lord grant that each of you will find rest in the home of another husband."

Then she kissed them goodbye and they wept aloud and said to her, "We will go back with you to your people."

But Naomi said, "Return home, my daughters. Why would you come with me? Am I going to have any more sons, who could become your husbands?

Return home, my daughters; I am too old to have another husband. Even if I thought there was still hope for me—even if I had a husband tonight and then gave birth to sons—would you wait until they grew up? Would you remain unmarried for them? No, my daughters. It is more bitter for me than for you, because the Lord's hand has turned against me!"

At this they wept aloud again. Then Orpah kissed her mother-in-law goodbye, but Ruth clung to her.

"Look," said Naomi, "your sister-in-law is going back to her people and her gods. Go back with her."

But Ruth replied, "Don't urge me to leave you or to turn back from you. Where you go I will go, and where you stay I will stay. Your people will be my people and your God my God. Where you die I will die, and there I will be buried. May the Lord deal with me, be it ever so severely, if even death separates you and me." When Naomi realized that Ruth was determined to go with her, she stopped urging her.

So the two women went on until they came to Bethlehem. When they arrived in Bethlehem, the whole town was stirred because of them, and the women exclaimed, "Can this be Naomi?"

"Don't call me Naomi," she told them. "Call me Mara, because the Almighty has made my life very bitter. I went away full, but the Lord has brought me back empty. Why call me Naomi? The Lord has afflicted me; the Almighty has brought misfortune upon me."

So Naomi returned from Moab accompanied by Ruth the Moabite, her daughter-in-law, arriving in Bethlehem as the barley harvest was beginning (Ruth 1: 1-20).

STUDY QUESTIONS

1. What did Ruth see in Naomi to merit her loyalty?
2. How might Naomi's and Ruth's shared hardships have strengthened their loyalty?
3. What characteristics have you developed through your hardships?
4. Grief often skews our thinking when we experience great loss. In what ways was your thinking clouded, even skewed after your loss?
5. What suggestions would you give to a new widow or any other person experiencing hard times, regarding her thinking shortly after her loss?

THINKING IT OVER

Sometimes meanings of names give us insights into persons, even expectations. Consider the meanings of names in the Book of Ruth.

Elimelek means "my God is king."

The name Mahlon appears to be derived from the verb (hala), meaning to be "weak," "sick," or "wounded"; "sickly."

Kilion means "failing," "unsuccessful."

Ruth means "friendship."

Certainly Naomi suffered. God sees, understands, and acts.

> And the God of all grace, who called you to his eternal glory in Christ, after you have suffered a little while, will himself restore you and make you strong, firm and steadfast (I Pt. 5: 10).

Remember that God, Who is grace-filled, is a restoration expert!

> May your unfailing love be my comfort, according to your promise to your servant (Ps. 119: 76).

You don't know whether the door is open or closed until you at least step up to the door.

PRACTICAL APPLICATION

1. What strengths have you gained as a result of your loss?
2. What new blessings has God brought into your life after your loss?
3. Accept new challenges, not as failure or setbacks, but as opportunities to change.

SIX

COURAGEOUS
Ruth

The Book of Ruth

We were friends from our childhood. I was always the courageous one, though Orpah was a bit older. When Orpah stepped back, I stepped forward. When Orpah was silent, I spoke. We were related, which meant celebration times were shared. She was content to skip in our courtyards. I always wanted to venture and explore. I loved climbing the limestone hills, feeling the cool grass under my bare feet. The views from the high plateaus were endless. I liked to imagine life beyond Kir.

Entering our teen years we spent more time learning the tasks of women. I missed those adventures of investigating beyond the community, but we were expected to marry. We needed to be prepared.

Orpah was not surprised when I suggested we meet two young Jewish men. She was accustomed to me bringing different ideas and different people into our lives. I was glad to have a friend like her, steady and predictable. I loved her look of surprise when we ventured farther than our familiar areas.

This Jewish family had boys who had become respected carpenters in Kir. Our families increasingly included them in celebrations and feast times. They never entered our temples. But we shared meals and were permitted, even encouraged, to talk with them. We were learning that some young men were foolhardy, some were dependable, some had potential, and some did not. These young men, given their family business, were seen as desirable husbands.

What started as polite conversations developed into intrigue. While shared times were in the presence of adults, I eagerly listened as Mahlon spoke of his family traditions, which they only practiced in their home. Orpah and Kilion often listened as I questioned Mahlon with curiosity. I hungered for something more, something beyond my people, their traditions. Orpah was content. We both were drawn to a common characteristic in these young men. They honored their mother. They spoke differently from other young men, never brash or vulgar. And they listened as well.

I was not surprised when our marriages were ultimately arranged. I was eager to begin life with Mahlon. Orpah would probably have waited. But given that the men were brothers and Orpah and I close, not only in age but in friendship, our marriages would be combined. The anticipation of our marriages was marred by the unexpected death of Elimelek. Through the sadness and mourning, again these brothers' love and care for their mother was evident.

After an appropriate time, the day of our marriages finally arrived. It was a great celebration. My father provided lambs and choice calves for roasting. The absence of Mahon and Kilion's father was evident, but their mother, Naomi, provided her most delicious loaves. Different from our tradition, but savored by all.

We honored their traditions by offering no sacrifices to Baal or Chemosh to bless our unions. As was their tradition, our marriages were consummated in the homes of our fathers. While I found this strange, I simply wanted to be Mahlon's wife. Afterward we moved into their family home.

Three women sharing the same cooking area was common. But Naomi's practices were—well, challenging. It seemed as though countless rules were invented, unnecessary and without reason. Yet Naomi's gentle spirit and willingness to teach endeared her to both of us.

Thankfully, our husbands discerned that a separate space for her would be better. They were able to purchase a small lot next to us. I think Naomi was grateful to be on her own. We saw her daily, even joined her to share lunch. Our husbands adapted to our habits. We did not need to heed the endless strange cooking rules Naomi not only followed, but cherished.

It concerned me that neither of our husbands became robust men. They had neither the appetites of Moabite men, nor the stamina. What they lacked in strength, they made up for in persistence.

All of these surprised me a bit, but no surprise was greater than the fact that neither I nor Orpah were becoming pregnant. Neither Orpah nor I would ever speak of intimate things, but we shared knowing, sad glances as each month our barrenness was confirmed.

Could it be that our marriage celebrations were ten years ago? The early years had flown by. But time seemed to move more slowly. Both Kilion and Mahlon shrank physically. They were unable to keep pace with building orders the way they had earlier. Naomi noticed. I knew she was concerned.

She invited me to her home one hot afternoon. Her room was stifling. I invited her to our courtyard under the shade of a tamarisk bush. There was a bit of breeze there. We sat. I could see the expectant look on her face. She glanced about to assure me that no one else would hear our conversation. I knew important words would be shared. For the first time, Naomi spoke of the births of her sons. She folded her hands in her lap and began.

———

"The joy of giving birth to my first son was mixed with concern. He was not a ruddy, robust babe, but rather thin with pronounced eyes and nose and no chubby cheeks. Elimelek named him Mahlon, meaning to be weak, sick, an apt name for the moment, one I hoped would prove to be untrue of his life. I devoted every fiber of my being to his health. He seemed to want to nurse constantly. I would have gladly given all my energy to my dear Mahlon. But unexpectedly I was soon pregnant again. It was as if my body could not nourish both Mahlon and the babe growing inside me.

"Labor pangs came unexpectedly, a month before they should have. Kilion's birth was so long I even wondered if I would survive. Eventually he emerged. I was too exhausted to notice his condition, just grateful he was not lifeless as I half expected. I was told I fainted with exhaustion. When I awoke, Elimelek stroked my damp head and told me he named our second son.

'Kilion is his name. He struggles to breathe, but he grasps my finger strongly. They will both grow to be strong men.'

"I took comfort from his words."

———

Naomi studied my face intently as if looking to see whether I understood her words. I nodded, not knowing what to think or say. I realized this wise woman recognized the changes in her sons these recent months. Did she have foreknowledge of something, or was it a foolish sense of foreboding?

I had known Naomi long enough to respect her wisdom. Had she not guided her family with steady resolve after the death of her husband? Didn't her sons trust her completely to guide them in the business? She knew, understood, and explained what her husband would have wanted them to know. I took her worn hands and pressed them to my check. I thanked her and we parted, she to sleep and me to complete a rough garment I was making for Mahlon.

I wondered what our kinsmen thought of the reality that we bore no children. Did the gods look with disfavor on us because we had not married within our own clan? Words were never spoken. But we became distant from our relatives. Cousins were raising their children. Our mothers held grandchildren. Not ours.

Mahlon changed his habit of returning to work after the heat of midday. I was not surprised. He struggled more to breathe each day. One night I was awakened by a strange sound from his lips. It was a rattling sound, ragged and unsettling. I bent over him and realized I was watching life leave his frail body. I could only stare, dry-eyed. I had known this was coming.

Days after we buried Mahlon, Kilion injured himself while shaping a beam with his ax. The infection, which most would have survived, brought a raging fever. No mixture of herbs contained it. He died. We buried him beside his brother. The mound from Mahlon's grave had not yet flattened.

Orpah and I clung ever more to each other. We traveled together a road few traveled. Marrying foreigners, loving them, following the strange traditions Naomi insisted upon, thankfully only briefly. And then we both became young widows. Burying our husbands, experiencing our own people distancing themselves from us. Intentional? Oblivious? We did not know. Few embraced us in our loss. We felt like outsiders in our own town.

———

Through all this, Ruth came to admire Naomi greatly. She knew what she believed, Who she believed in. She treasured people, life, her two daughters-in-law though they cooked different foods, and followed traditions unlike her Jewish habits. But life in Moab without their men was not sustainable.

What followed was common in the lives of widows. First they sold the tools of the carpentry business, food for a few more months. What now? Could their homes be sold, or would they be taken? Three widows had no means or power to defend themselves. Ruth noted a look of resolve in Naomi's eyes.

Naomi decided to return home.

The road to Bethlehem was neither safe nor easy. But what choice did two young widows have? The young women started the journey with their mother-in-law. Ruth could tell Naomi was uneasy. With each step toward home, her face appeared more troubled. Ruth knew she'd soon speak her mind. And she did.

Naomi was telling them to leave her—to go back home! How could this mother-in-law, who accepted them with all their strange ways, now urge them to go back to their parents? They objected. But finally Naomi prevailed—with Orpah. Custom dictated that Ruth go back also. Return to her own people. But Ruth was courageous. She refused.

The road to Bethlehem was challenging, exciting, and more difficult than I imagined. I could sense Orpah's growing anxiety. She was not as strong as I, neither of body, nor spirit, for taking on hard things. When Naomi urged us to go back, I was not surprised when Orpah relented. We clung to each other and wept. I did not try to dissuade her. Watching her turn, seeing my friend from childhood take those steps toward home, I was not tempted to join her. Yet I was profoundly sad. Another loss—my husband and now my dearest friend.

Orpah will be fine, I told myself. I watched until her image grew small. Her family would welcome her. All would be well. I turned to see Naomi studying me intently. I walked briskly toward her and never looked back. Orpah faced our familiar Moab; I faced the unknown.

Thankfully, I could trust Naomi to know the journey. She amazed me, for although she was older she approached the steep cliff ascent with boldness and the wilderness roads as if they were hers for the taking.

I came to know her more intimately as we walked. She remembered. She told stories of her family's pilgrimage on each road we traveled. I learned about her by watching her. Once stoic, she opened her soul more to me with each step. How could I do anything less than embrace her fully as my own and only family?

More importantly, I decided to embrace her God. It was not just Naomi's words of Him, His promises, His plans and provisions. It was seeing God in her. I had never experienced such direct faith, such honest questioning.

And then the complete comfort and encouragement God gave her was nothing like what my family believed. Her God was not forever angry, forever changing what He demanded. I claimed her God as my God, and my Lord.

Entering Bethlehem was strange, bittersweet for her mother-in-law. People approached them, questioned, and stared at Ruth. Ruth was surprised, even a bit proud, that Naomi treated her more like her daughter than daughter-in-law.

Some looked at her with complete disdain, no doubt reminding themselves of the wickedness of the Moabites, their refusal to welcome their ancestors into this land. Regardless of Naomi's standing in the community, Ruth would forever be "Other,"—in fact, despised.

———

We were allowed to stay in what was once Elimelek's home. Shelter, even crumbling and in need of repair, was better than the road back from Moab. Naomi began instructing me in the ways of her people, the traditions of family land, provisions for widows, orphans, and aliens. I listened, not understanding these strange traditions, but trusting Naomi.

She explained God's arrangement of providing for the poor by gleaning the edges of the fields. The harvesters were instructed to let those in need glean and not starve. It was hard work for sure. It must have humbled her profoundly to be a poor widow in her own land.

"Let me go to the fields," I insisted. Finally, a way I could give back to Naomi. I could provide for her, as her son once did for me.

I arose early and walked to the barley fields. I knew no one, so I just entered a field. I covered myself as best I could, hoping to blend in with the other young women gleaning the edges of the field. I wondered how many were young widows as I was, ushered into poverty by the deaths of our husbands. I noticed the harvesters often stared over long at all of us. Some women met their gaze. I looked down, intent only on bringing as much as I could home that evening.

Eventually the common bond of working, bending, and perspiring in the extreme heat found us beginning to talk. My foreign status was immediately recognizable. They seemed not to care. Poverty linked us in ways the wealthy would never understand.

A voice boomed over the field. "The Lord be with you!" We all straightened. "It's Boaz, the owner of this field," the woman next to me whispered. "The Lord bless you!" his harvesters answered. This kind of greeting would never have been heard in Moab.

I bent over again, even more intent on gathering what I could. So intent was I that I did not notice his approach to me. His voice startled me. "My daughter, listen to me. Don't go and glean in another field and don't go away from here. Stay here with the women who work for me. Watch the field where the men are harvesting, and follow along after the women. I have told the men not to lay a hand on you. And whenever you are thirsty, go and get a drink from the water jars the men have filled." I pressed my face to the ground. "Why have I found such favor in your eyes that you notice me—a foreigner?" (Ruth 2: 9-10) The booming voice that greeted his harvesters was now soft, almost tender. "I've been told all about what you have done for your mother-in-law since the death of your husband—how you left your father and mother and your homeland and came to live with a people you did not know before. May the Lord repay you for what you have done. May you be richly rewarded by the Lord, the God of Israel, under whose wings you have come to take refuge" (Ruth 2: 11-12). It seemed the whole of Bethlehem knew my entire life. As I looked at Boaz, I did not realize, would never have known then, what I learned later. His mother was Rahab. No one spoke her name without adding her identity. Rahab was a harlot, a Canaanite, a woman who betrayed her city by hiding two Israeli spies on her rooftop. When the Israelites besieged her city, Jeri-cho, she and her family were spared. She, Rahab the harlot, married Salmon, the son of an esteemed leader of Israel. Boaz was their son. Surely this man looking at me with compassion knew something of the struggles of a foreigner among these strange people. I sensed his understanding. At the time I did not know why his heart was so tender toward the aliens among his people. His mother was "Other" just as I was.

I gushed my gratitude and wished to continue to find favor in his eyes, though my standing was less than a servant. I bent more vigorously to my task. The young girls around me whis-pered, "You're favored, you're favored." They seemed to believe some implied intention I did not detect. I trusted the heat of the day would camouflage my blushing cheeks.

As if the morning had not been full of the unexpected, Boaz asked me to join him at mealtime. I had not eaten until full for days and did so with gratitude. I tucked the abundance of my meal in my tunic. Naomi would be well satisfied this night. The afternoon was even more productive. At evening I entered our home with an ephah of grain. While that might have been a heavy load for some, carrying it home was easy compared to the road from Moab to Bethlehem.

Naomi listened, observed, and planned. She believed her God would find a way for this tenacious young woman. After all, Ruth loved her mother-in-law more intensely than Naomi could ever have imagined.

———

Naomi finished the abundance of my lunch, and eyed again the grain I brought home. She declared it was at least worth two weeks' wages. She looked at me with discernment. "Ruth, my precious daughter, we must find a home for you. Gleaning behind the harvesters is feeding us now. But we must find a way, a better way, a permanent place for you."

———

As the end of harvest time came, Naomi told Ruth to go to the threshing floor of Boaz, who was a relative. Winnowing out the grain was celebration time for the hard work of planting, tending, and finally harvesting. The men ate and drank in celebration and then slept on the floor. More than a convenient place to sleep, it was added safety for the grain belonging to each who shared the winnowing place. Not all could be trusted not to take from another's grain pile.

———

It seemed each tradition I learned was stranger than the one before. Naomi was asking me to dress in my best garments, perfume myself, and go to a threshing floor? Her request would have strained my trust in her had we not endured so much together.

I obediently put on my best clothing. Arriving at the threshing floor, I saw the activity of winnowing the grain filled the air with chaff blowing and piles of barley growing. I recognized a few women I gleaned with and stood with them. The feast was a celebration like none I had ever seen. Women did not eat with the harvesters, but were onlookers. I did not know why they came. I certainly would tell no one why I was here. I could hardly understand Naomi's instructions myself. I simply trusted her.

As night enveloped the revelers, weary from exertion and warmed with wine, they bedded down. I watched and waited until Boaz approached his great heap of grain and lay down to sleep. When I was certain he was sleeping, I silently tucked myself under his cover near his feet and waited. All was quiet but my pounding heart. This custom seemed strange and the threshing floor the strangest place on which this widow ever attempted sleep. In fact, I felt a greater sense of belonging sleeping on the hard road from Moab. My identity was simply a widow and a foreigner who did not belong here.

I could not sleep. Boaz rose slightly and shuffled a bit. It was midnight. His foot touched me. Surprised, yet quietly he whispered, "Who are you?"

Custom. This strange behavior was understood by both Naomi and Boaz. Naomi was reminding her relative Boaz that respecting her dead husband and sons meant providing for her and Ruth. She was sending Boaz a message that she and Ruth would accept his honoring their tradition of inheritance. She was challenging him, no, summoning him, to take action.

"I am Ruth, your servant; spread your cloak over your servant for you are next-of-kin"(Ruth 3: 9).

Boaz's words, whispered so as not to awaken those around him, are words etched into my memory. He praised my loyalty, loyalty to my new family's tradition, not the whims of a young widow. He declared this a greater pledge of loyalty than my words to Naomi on the road to Bethlehem. Then he called me "worthy!" Whatever was to follow, I would never forget that word describing me. Moabite, alien, widow, now worthy. I would wear my identity with humble pride.

He laid out his action plan. I listened and remembered, hoping for Naomi to bring light to my understanding for what lay ahead.

Before sunlight, while Ruth could leave under cover of darkness to protect her reputation, Boaz sent her back to Naomi with an exceedingly large gift of grain. Naomi knew his intention.

While the transaction the next morning at the public gate might have seemed strange to an outsider, all present understood what Boaz did. He declared his willingness to honor Naomi's family land and marry Ruth. All present added their acceptance of the transaction and wished him offspring. No doubt, a large and celebratory wedding followed.

I should have been weary from sleep deprivation from the long night before. But I was energized and paced as Naomi rehearsed what would be going on at the city gate. Boaz would invite our next of kin as he was passing by to sit with him.

Then he would ask ten elders of the city to join them. This was tradition, order, openness, the expected way to conduct business.

Boaz would tell them Naomi wanted to sell their land. Of course the next of kin would want that and nod his acceptance. Then Boaz would add that the widow of Naomi's eldest son, Mahlon, would be part of the acquisition. The next of kin would pause studying not just Boaz, but the elders. Thoughtfully he would consider his wife and sons and the impact on their inheritance. It would be his obligation to be husband to Ruth and bear sons to whom the land would later revert. His window of profit from farming the land would be short, and his own land would need to be divided with the additional sons.

I tired of listening to Naomi's explanations. Would the morning hours drag on forever? We heard a knock at the door.

Naomi opened it. Boaz stood smiling broadly, holding up a sandal. Naomi reached up hugging his neck, unrestrained.

Boaz, with only mildly subdued excitement, explained what happened. "Your next of kin recognized he would diminish his inheritance. He declined the purchase and offered me that right. Our verbal agreement was sealed. He took off his sandal and gave it to me."

I understood. I met Boaz's gaze with a nod of acceptance and assurance. I could love this man. He nodded slightly.

Boaz strode off with confident determination. My future was not in his hands. Though I trusted Boaz, I trusted my Lord God more.

Our marriage celebration was different even from those of his people. Although the bride's father is expected to host the celebration, this was impossible as I was an alien from Moab.

Naomi's poverty prevented her from any meaningful contribution. This did not matter at all to Boaz and his family. His mother and father hosted the great celebration in their compound, an immense space that contained Boaz's home as well. The courtyard was packed. Sheep were slaughtered and roasted, mounds of freshly baked loaves kept appearing on the tables, grapes, raisins, dried fruits, olives, and endless flowing wine filled the air with delicious scents of abundant food.

While I wished to remember every moment, every face, every greeting, my overwhelming memory was the nearness of Boaz. While he could have surrounded himself with his men folk, his friends, and relatives, he was constantly at my side. That memory gave rise to the source of the other great memory of the day. I no longer felt myself as "Other." I felt surrounded by my people.

Our marriage was consummated in Boaz's home that night. I secretly wondered if I was a barren woman. My question was soon answered. I delighted in the wave of nausea one morning! What woman would do that? One who had waited to be with child for more than a decade. Even as my steps grew heavy with the weight of our growing babe inside me, my heart floated each day with joy. Naomi hovered over much. But I could not blame her or refuse her care.

Obed was born into a gaggle of women who could not stop chattering to Naomi about his handsome form and the blessing he was to her in her aged widowhood. I simply looked on. Often the amazement of the past months was almost too much to fathom. I prayed to my God and my Lord. I thanked Him endlessly and profusely, and loved Boaz more than I could ever have imagined. That love was returned.

Boaz loved Ruth. Obed was born. Naomi's empty arms now cradled her grandson. Ruth's empty arms were filled with Boaz, Obed, and probably other children.

While this story shows that God's plans are often unexpected, unseen, and at times unwanted, Naomi and Ruth's story shows that He brings good in unexpected ways and from unexpected places. Yes, courage is required of us, and patience to allow His strong arms to work on our behalf.

STUDY GUIDE
THE BOOK OF RUTH

What would it take for you to leave your home country? Leave familiar neighbors, family, and food that are your way of life? Courage would be required, to be sure. Read the short Book of Ruth and you'll see a young woman who did all that—as a young widow.

Was it because of her new mother-in-law's bright and engaging personality that drew her to follow Naomi to a strange land? Hardly. Naomi was distraught, suffering her own grief of widowhood. Grief does keep us from seeing even the glimmers of positives in our lives. Yet Ruth saw in Naomi a quality of tenacious faith and desire to return to her roots that drew Ruth to be one courageous young woman. Courageous, yes. But still willing to listen and heed the advice of her mother-in-law:

One day Ruth's mother-in-law Naomi said to her, "My daughter, I must find a home for you, where you will be well provided for. Now Boaz, with whose women you have worked, is a relative of ours. Tonight he will be winnowing barley on the threshing floor. Wash, put on perfume, and get dressed in your best clothes. Then go down to the threshing floor, but don't let him know you are there until he has finished eating and drinking. When he lies down, note the place where he is lying. Then go and uncover his feet and lie down. He will tell you what to do"(Ruth 3: 1-4).

When Ruth came to her mother-in-law, Naomi asked, "How did it go, my daughter?"

Then she told her everything Boaz had done for her and added, "He gave me these six measures of barley, saying, 'Don't go back to your mother-in-law empty-handed.'"

Then Naomi said, "Wait, my daughter, until you find out what happens. For the man will not rest until the matter is settled today" (Ruth 3: 16-18).

Then Boaz announced to the elders and all the people, "Today you are witnesses that I have bought from Naomi all the property of Elimelek, Kilion and Mahlon. I have also acquired Ruth the Moabite, Mahlon's widow, as my wife, in order to maintain the name of the dead with his property, so that his name will not disappear from among his family or from his hometown. Today you are witnesses!"

Then the elders and all the people at the gate said, "We are witnesses. May the Lord make the woman who is coming into your home like Rachel and Leah, who together built up the family of Israel. May you have standing in Ephrathah and be famous in Bethlehem. Through the offspring the Lord gives you by this young woman, may your family be like that of Perez, whom Tamar bore to Judah."

So Boaz took Ruth and she became his wife. When he made love to her, the Lord enabled her to conceive, and she gave birth to a son. The women said to Naomi: "Praise be to the Lord, who this day has not left you without a guardian-redeemer. May he become famous throughout Israel! He will renew your life and sustain you in your old age. For your daughter-in-law, who loves you and who is better to you than seven sons, has given him birth."

Then Naomi took the child in her arms and cared for him. The women living there said, "Naomi has a son!" And they named him Obed. He was the father of Jesse, the father of David (Ruth 4: 9-17).

STUDY QUESTIONS

1. Have you wondered on becoming a widow, if God still has a plan for you? You may find this applicable and helpful whether you're a widow or not.

2. What actions did Ruth take that showed she had
   courage?
3. What change after your loss has been the most
   difficult to manage?

THINKING IT OVER

When the future and outcomes are unknown, we can become
fearful and distracted. God's Word speaks clearly regarding His
plans for us.

> Finally, be strong in the Lord and in his mighty power
> (Eph. 6: 10).

> ...because you know that the testing of your faith
> produces perseverance (James 1: 3).

> I cry out to God Most High, to God, who fulfills [His
> purpose] for me (Ps. 57: 2).

> The LORD will fulfill his purpose for me; your love,
> O LORD, endures for ever—do not abandon the
> works of your hands (Ps. 138: 8).

God numbers our days and is the giver of life:

> ...your eyes saw my unformed body.
> All the days ordained for me
> were written in your book
> before one of them came to be (Ps. 139: 16).

PERSONAL APPLICATION

1. What challenges do you see ahead for which you do not yet see a solution?
2. What people in your trusted circle could help you navigate this challenge?
3. While you are waiting to see God's plan unfold, write a gratitude list of what He has done so far.

SEVEN

PRAYERFUL
Anna, the Widow
Who Prayed

Luke 2: 36-38

"What will become of me now?" The edges of young Anna's soul curled, her heart thudded as tears spilled over her widow's shawl. Seven years of marriage, only twenty-five years old, childless, and she had already buried her husband.

Tradition meant some relative could marry her. Her heart recoiled at the thought. There had been, and was, only one love of her life, and he lay cold in the family tomb. She kept his tunic, spread it over her bed each night, and wept into its folds, breathing in the scent of the one who had loved her.

But that would fade. The future became the present. Reality began to push through her grief and demand to be addressed. What now?

———

My family believed the prophets who came before us. My father was a devout follower, believing there would be a Messiah. I grew up hearing his words. He quoted the prophet Micah.

"But you, Bethlehem Ephrathah, though you are small among the clans of Judah, out of you will come for me one who will be ruler over Israel, whose origins are from of old, from ancient times" (Mic. 5: 2).

My father explained that Micah also said many nations would come to him, he would settle disputes, there would be peace.

I could not imagine such a life. Our people were oppressed by the Romans. We were taxed and cheated. Many of my people served them as slaves. The Romans believed their leader was a god to be worshipped. This idea was abhorrent to our people.

Living under Roman rule, even as a child I sensed fear when a Roman soldier would ride through our tiny street. My mother would hurry us inside. Tension and distrust were palpable. My father spoke with longing that our Messiah would come soon.

I could quote Micah's words and the prophet Isaiah also. "See, a king will reign in righteousness and rulers will rule with justice" (Is. 32: 1).

"A shoot will come up from the stump of Jesse; from his roots a Branch will bear fruit"(Is. 11: 1).

How different from our world ruled by the Romans. They believed in science, wealth, social standing, and power. Our people could only exist with their permission. I heard of a group called the Zealots who led waves of revolt. While many understood their anger, their efforts were futile. They were brutally killed by soldiers who delighted in torturing before killing their enemies.

With sadness I began to see the Roman influence within my own people. Rather than a unified people, wealth and power caused divisions among us.

My father encouraged me to think beyond, see beyond to the day our Messiah would come.

I admired and loved my father greatly. He taught me as if I were his son. The older I got, the more I noticed my friends were not being taught as I was. Their brothers, yes, but not them.

I hungered to learn. My father took me to the temple to hear the Torah read. I remembered these passages. Though Rome was crushing my people, I had hope. Our Messiah would come.

As was our tradition, I married. Father chose wisely. He was a good man, much older, but established and able to provide a small dwelling near the temple. He knew my hunger and honored my desire to spend as much time there as I could. While each year we wished and prayed for children without an answer, I believed God would open my womb. My husband's untimely death was a greater loss for me than most because we had no children. The days following my time of mourning seemed purposeless. I took note of male relatives looking at me. I knew their thoughts. "Who will take her as his wife to raise sons to honor her husband?"

I wanted no other. In fact, I knew from the Torah that God's heart was tender toward widows. I announced to my father that I had made a vow to God. I would not marry, but spend my life praying, fasting, and worshipping Him. He accepted this and was my spokesperson to my husband's family. What could they say? I had made my vow before God. Other women before me did that—with God's resulting blessing.

With what little I had, and help from my father, I acquired a tiny abode near the women's gate of the temple. Every morning I prepared a small fire, heated my tiny clay pot, and pressed the dough I prepared into the hot inside. Once it baked, I would carefully peel it off and savor it.

Wrapping myself in my widow's cloak, I entered the court of the Gentiles, circled to the fourteen steps leading to the women's court. There I knelt and thanked God for keeping me through another night and providing for me. Then I rose and walked among the people, carefully studying their faces. Couples walked in bringing their new babes for the rite of purification. They first brought their currency to the moneychangers since sacrificial animals could only be purchased with Hebrew shekels.

Then they purchased a bird or other animal for sacrifice. Only then could they approach the area where sacrifice could be made for purification of babies. A priest would come down the fourteen steps from the Gate of Nicanor to perform the rite.

I rose earlier every day and entered the temple. Thankfully, there I could escape the stares of the Roman guards. When I was on the streets outside the temple, marked by my widow's garb and youth, their looks sent more than a ripple of apprehension through my body. I feared them even more than I had as a small child. I prayed and recited God's words back to Him. I loved being in the temple. Its sights and sounds were comfort and safety. I stayed later each night.

I spent most of my time in the women's area. I was especially drawn to women who came there alone. Before hearing many of them praying, I sensed their longing, much like mine before my widowhood. Kneeling beside them I joined them in praying for a child. It was not uncommon for them to abruptly become silent, look closely into my face, and then cling to me weeping in gratitude that someone understood their longing. How often I watched that young woman leave, face wet with tears, but with more peace than when she entered.

I found great satisfaction in praying with my people. Going back to my tiny abode, I prayed on, interceding for each one.

I began to see the plight of the poor among us. The moneychangers, our very own people, took advantage of them. Blemished turtledoves and lambs were sold to them. They incurred debt, anger, and humiliation trying to follow the customs expected of them.

How could I more fully enter the reality of their lives? They often lacked food. I determined to fast regularly, to take the gnawing sensation as God's call back to prayer. I began to learn that the demands of the body should be subjected to God's invitation to be satisfied with Him alone.

Each morning I still baked my loaf, or sometimes two, enjoying the aroma. My stomach growled, but I did not eat. I prayed for God to show me to whom I should give my loaves that day. He never failed in prompting me to see a person, or couple, poverty etched in their faces as well as on display in their worn garments. They would enjoy a fine fresh loaf today. I sensed satisfaction greater than a full stomach. They would invite me to sit with them, which I gladly did.

Often they poured out their troubles. I would remind them of God's promise to our people. "Our Messiah will come! Don't lose hope." I prayed for their comfort and protection while in their presence and through the night in my small home. My contentment grew. My prayers of gratitude tumbled over my petitions for God's protection for my people.

The priests took note that I was in the temple day and night. One of my great delights as the months and years passed was seeing women with whom I'd prayed enter the temple with a babe in their arms. They would hurry to me. We would praise God together, full of joy.

Others I prayed for and shared loaves with sought me out when they returned. Their poverty might still be evident, but hope was rising. And there is immeasurable wealth in hope.

As I prayed, my God helped me remember even more of what I learned of the Torah and the Books of the Prophets. One theme seemed to grip my mind and my heart more than any other: the Messiah. I began to recall the prophet Isaiah's predictions. I pondered them and asked God to show me more, teach me more. He answered.

In fact, on occasion as I was praying, He would prompt me to look at a specific person. A strange but certain sense would come over me. He would give me words to say to that person. At first I felt a twinge of fear. What if that word of prediction did not come true? My heart would break to disappoint or mislead one of my people. The sense engulfed me. *Be obedient, my child.*

I had no choice. I spoke His words to whomever He directed.

While I did not know the outcome of all the words I spoke to others, I knew some. I only spoke when that strong sense of God directed me. And every word I spoke came true.

My people were beginning to consider me a prophet. The priests began to take note that I was always there, and I had the respect of our people. I had their permission to stay in the Court of the Nazarites overnight.

What would seem like long years to most passed quickly. I found myself needing less grain and oil to sustain myself. Yet God provided more. I had more to bring to those in hunger. Fasting was no deprivation compared to the joy of blessing the hungry with food.

I was thankful for the familiarity of the temple. My passion for the Messiah grew. "How soon, Lord, before you send Him?" I yearned for that day. At the same time, I realized my life would soon be over. If He came today, I would have little time to live under His reign, let alone follow Him as He traveled and taught. I would have little time to see Him restore justice. I would have little time to revel freely in safe streets. When I was tempted with despair, I quickly turned to prayers of gratitude. Always my heart soared again.

I spent more time in the Court of the Gentiles. What compassion I felt for those praying there. Some believed our God was the true God. But they could not fully enter our customs. As I knelt and prayed for them, that strong sense enveloped me. "Child of mine, go to the women's court." I rose and attempted to hurry up those fourteen steps.

A young, plain, and evidently poor couple stood before the priest with their infant. My breath fairly left me. I clutched my cloak to still my shaking hands.

There before me was the Messiah. A babe for sure with nothing to distinguish him from any other babe. I knew without being told he was of the house of Jesse and he was born in Bethlehem. This I knew.

I also knew how He would live, how He would lead, and how He would die. What seemed like a long time was but moments. My body froze in place, His life moved through my mind. I remembered long passages of descriptions of His life, even His death.

Finally I approached them, giving loud thanks to God. His mother and earthly father heard my words with simple looks of trust. They seemed neither alarmed nor surprised.

From that day on I could discern those coming in the temple who were truly looking forward to the redemption of my dear Jerusalem. Some came because it was custom. Others came sharing my anticipation. I told them, "He has come. I've seen the babe that is our Messiah." We rejoiced.

Those with whom I had shared my loaves sought me out, as did many others I could hardly remember. They reminded me of my prayers for them. For many, I brought them hope in ways no other could. Widowed and childless, they saw in me that hope is from God alone, not from the abundance of your life.

They found her one night just inside the Court of the Gentiles near the women's gate. Some believed age took her life. Others believed she intentionally breathed her last asking God for not one more day. She had seen Him, her Messiah. This earth held nothing more for her.

They tenderly took her frail, gnarled body and laid her in the family tomb near her husband. More noteworthy than the fact of Anna's death was the fact that she had truly lived.

Anna's life stands out among women in the Bible as she defied the traditions of her time. Remaining single after being widowed and being a female prophet was not the norm. We don't know her living conditions, only that she never left the temple. She was a prophetess, so we assume she had her own small living space in the temple compound. How did she sustain herself? Was she fed from the tithes and offerings people brought to the temple? We know none of those specifics. Simply that she made a choice: her purpose in life would be to worship, fast, and pray every day of her life.

Worship is familiar. We can imagine ourselves worshipping with Anna. Though we express ourselves in different ways in different cultures, we tell God of our love for Him. With our acceptance of the life He gives us, whether quietly on bended knee, or dancing with tambourines, we worship.

We pray. Perhaps not as frequently or fervently as Anna did, but prayer is common to our faith. Prayers of thanksgiving, petition, and admiration: quietly, publicly, in solitude, in multitudes, we pray.

Fasting is not so prevalent. Or perhaps it is, but seldom mentioned since Scripture admonishes us to fast privately. What benefit is fasting?

Fasting tells our body its demands are secondary to our spiritual well-being.

Fasting focuses us on prayer. Our stomach rumbles as we go about our day. Reminder! This is a day I have set aside to pray.

I imagine one of Anna's questions for her Lord in the early days of her widowhood included, "What is my purpose now?" Wife, mother, those dreams, those expectations were over. What now?

She chose a most noble cause, one anyone can embrace. You need not be wealthy, or healthy, popular, or high-profile to devote yourself to worship, prayer, and fasting. This focus in Anna's life resulted in her being one of the four female prophets listed in Scripture, a noble calling to be sure.

While she had prophesied before, no doubt her words to her listeners were more intense, more intentional after seeing the Messiah. "I have seen the Christ Child! He is born! He will be our Redeemer!" She was in the temple at the time Joseph and Mary brought baby Jesus. Immediate recognition! This prophetess announced the Christ child. At the age of eighty-four, no doubt she had a new energy, a new passion, a new reason to worship more passionately, pray more fervently, and fast with even greater focus. Her eyes saw, and she was able to announce that the Savior, for whom all her people were waiting, was born!

Are you seeking focus in your life? Consider the life of Anna. She is an example for us all.

STUDY GUIDE
LUKE 2: 36-38

If we want to be more Christ-like, one priority is to pray. Fervently, frequently, focused. Any time, anywhere, any reason. I love the example of Anna. One of the four female prophets of

Scripture, she was married for seven years, and then widowed. She never left the temple. The result: she was there when Mary and Joseph brought baby Jesus to be consecrated. She was old at that time. Years of waiting, years of praying, years of fasting rewarded. An excellent example, my friend. Pray on.

> There was also a prophet, Anna, the daughter of Penuel, of the tribe of Asher. She was very old; she had lived with her husband seven years after her marriage, and then was a widow until she was eighty-four. She never left the temple but worshiped night and day, fasting and praying. Coming up to them at that very moment, she gave thanks to God and spoke about the child to all who were looking forward to the redemption of Jerusalem (Lk. 2: 36-38).

Scripture is clear that widows may chose to remarry or chose to remain single. Abigail was a widow who remarried (I Sam. 25). Anna, after becoming a widow, chose to remain single.

STUDY QUESTIONS

1. Why might some widows chose to remarry?
2. Why might some widows chose to remain single?
3. What are the dangers of seeking solutions and comfort from another person?
4. How did God use Anna in her widowhood?

THINKING IT OVER

No doubt prophetess Anna brought comfort to many who came to the Temple. Through fasting and prayer, she touched God's heart and moved His hands on behalf of many.

While some might see her life as small and restricted, consider God's Word.

> But godliness with contentment is great gain (I Tm. 6: 6).

> But if we have food and clothing, we will be content with that (I Tm. 6: 8).

> Keep your lives free from the love of money and be content with what you have, because God has said, "Never will I leave you; never will I forsake you" (Heb. 13: 5).

> I know what it is to be in need, and I know what it is to have plenty. I have learned the secret of being content in any and every situation, whether well fed or hungry, whether living in plenty or in want (Phil. 4: 12).

Anna passed on God's comfort to many. And she did so as a "vintage" woman through age eighty-four! Consider that God's greatest moment of honor and opportunity for Him to use you may be yet to come!

PERSONAL APPLICATION

1. Have you sensed God's attention to you? In what ways?
2. What are your sources of comfort?
3. What are your opportunities to give comfort away?
4. What additional challenges come from remarriage?
5. Talk openly, frankly, and listen carefully to wise people regarding any person you may consider marrying.

EIGHT

TENACITY/ DETERMINATION
Mary, the Mother of Jesus

Luke 1: 26-38
Jesus' Birth and Childhood

Mary skipped to the well with her empty pot. Sixteen, betrothed to Joseph, who was a bit older, she was still a young girl inside in those moments of freedom. She and her friends talked and laughed as they filled their water pots. Hoisting hers on her head, the act reminded Mary that days of freedom like this would soon end. She would be married, have greater responsibilities, and soon have children.

But she was ready. This was their tradition and Joseph was a good man. His strong carpenter hands would provide for their children. Life would be simple, but good.

She listened well as her father quoted the Torah and the prophets to their family. Mary always had a unique hunger for the spiritual, truth you could count on, wise counsel. She hungered for the day when prophecy for her people would be fulfilled. God had promised them, promised her, that one day their Messiah would be born and free them from bondage.

She puzzled over what that might be. Freedom from the Romans? Prosperity instead of poverty? Her pondering would have to wait. She entered her home to her mother's calls for help with the endless chores of family life. That evening her family would meet with Joseph's family to plan their wedding. She would be able to see Joseph, listen as he spoke, imagine what their life together would be like.

A new day! Mary rose to go to the well. She was early and few others were about. She turned aside for a few moments, hoping her friends would arrive. Instead a beautiful creature appeared.

While this creature's beauty was beyond description, I was struck even more profoundly by the sense of his power, holiness, and wisdom.

I knew from my father's teaching that our God did sometimes send messages through angels. I breathed deeply waiting to hear his words, anticipation tinged with a bit of fear.

"Greetings, you who are highly favored! The Lord is with you" (Lk. 1: 30).

While those words sounded comforting, I still remembered that sometimes angels brought words of judgment. The angel noticed my distress and quickly reassured me that I need not be afraid. I simply listened. In a mere few minutes he told me words about myself I could hardly fathom.

I had found favor with God.

I would bear a son.

I would name him Jesus.

This I could understand. Then this beautiful creature continued.

"He will be great and will be called the Son of the Most High. The Lord God will give him the throne of his father David, and he will reign over Jacob's descendants forever; his kingdom will never end" (Lk. 1: 32-33).

He will be great, be called the Son of the Most High.

He will have the throne of David.

His kingdom will never end.

I could not help but respectfully question. In my mind I could not grasp "Son of the Most High" instead of son of Joseph. I had to ask.

How can this be? I'm a virgin.

He answered with words even more difficult to comprehend. Yet, I had always been taught that all things were possible with my God. This creature reassured me, telling me my relative Elizabeth was with child. My aged cousin! How could I doubt the ability of God to accomplish anything in any way?

I could only answer in barely a whisper. "I am the Lord's servant, May your word to me be fulfilled" (Lk. 1: 38).

And then he was gone.

Somehow seeing my friends at the well was no longer important. I stayed riveted to the spot. I rehearsed carefully what I had been told. I would become pregnant. I would bear a son and call him Jesus.

While this seemed impossible to grasp, his next words were even more difficult to fathom. Was it wrong to question? This beautiful creature seemed approachable. Being a virgin and giving birth to a son? I had continued listening.

All I'd heard seemed a jumble in my mind. I rehashed every phrase.

My mind hung on the impossible. I had questioned the beautiful creature, an act requiring courage. "How could this be?" Should I have been so bold? The angel answered. While I could not comprehend fully how I would become pregnant, the angel's gentle voice was reassuring. My answer was simple, yet profound. There was only one response. "I am the Lord's servant," I recalled. "May your word to me be fulfilled."

I willed myself to return to the task at hand.

———

She went slowly to the well. She saw her friends, but wanted to hurry through the task, rush home. Who would she talk to? Who would believe her?

Her God had a plan, but He did not show her all of that plan.

———

For days, I spoke to no one about this event. My family met again with Joseph's, this time just to share a meal. Wedding plans were already made. Our shared meal was a peaceful event except for my racing heart. I looked intently at Joseph. He met my gaze respectfully as always. But there was no hint of recognition of what I knew would shake not only our marriage, but the lives of all those about us. I felt I would burst trying to keep all I knew within me.

I remembered the beautiful creature's words about my relative Elizabeth. I would go to her! My parents consented to my travel. Surely my mother had noticed that I had become more quiet these days.

The walk into the hill country was soothing to my soul. Ordinary sights; sheep and their shepherd resting under a tree in the heat of the day. Soft clouds shaping and reshaping themselves. Ordinary was good. I would later look back on that three-day journey as one of the most peaceful, freedom-filled times in my life.

I entered Zechariah's home. Elizabeth was indeed with child. A miracle for sure. She hugged me mightily and spoke words of confirmation about all that was happening to me. My babe would be cousin to the babe who leaped in her womb when I entered their home. Zechariah was unable to speak at that time, but his kind look of approval was all I needed.

A weight that had been restricting the joy I should have experienced at this great news was lifted. Praise burst from within me with the freedom of Elizabeth's acceptance.

I stayed with Elizabeth for three months. She was grateful as her aged pregnancy slowed her much. My babe began to change my appearance. She and Zechariah were accepting, a gift I knew would be unlikely when I returned home.

Weeks went by. My betrothed, Joseph, learned of my pregnancy. It was expected and permitted that he put aside our engagement silently so as not to insult my family. He was a good man. Stares in our village burned my soul. No doubt his as well. I simply left this matter in God's hands. What choice did I have? People would choose to believe what they wished.

Thankfully, my parents and siblings did not shun me. I explained as best I could that an angel had appeared and told me I would bear a son. I did not reveal the whole message. Who would believe I would bear the Messiah? I could hardly embrace that myself. Zechariah came and sat with my father. He revealed the angel's visit to his wife and himself with a now renewed voice of confidence and faith unlike anything he ever experienced. His support and the knowledge of their miraculous son's birth brought our families together. Expectation with reservations? That understates our family at that time.

God visited Joseph, telling him of the upcoming birth of our Messiah. He came to my family asking that we begin our lives together without the usual celebration. They gratefully agreed. Joseph proved himself again, as he would many times in the years to come, that he was a man of faith and honor. When confronted in our village, he simply stated that I was his wife.

Later, he told me of specific instructions the angel brought to him. Some of my friends looked at me with pity. No celebration! No tradition to remember and tell generations to come. Others looked at me with disdain. I could not blame them.

We had a simple ceremony of marriage, but we did not physically come together until after Jesus' birth. What a turbulent way for our marriage to begin. But we both knew we were each chosen for the task. Which meant, leaning on God, we could accomplish His plan for our family. I would be the best mother I could be. Joseph would be the best adoptive father he could be.

Our family followed tradition. Tradition ruled above comfort and convenience. We never questioned that we would travel to

Bethlehem at the time of the census. We were unprepared for the throngs packing the small town. I was exhausted beyond belief from the trip, being near my babe's birthing time. Surely Joseph could find us a room. Surely any innkeeper would see my condition and find some small accommodation. Joseph knocked at yet another door. Our donkey thudded to the ground and I sat leaning against him. Was it fatigue causing the pain in my back? Joseph was returning and I could tell by how he walked that what he could offer was not what he wished. We were welcome to stay in a small cave that stabled the innkeeper's animals. Safe, somewhat protected, and all that was possible.

As labor pangs intensified that night, the reality of our babe's identity was pushed back as Joseph became my midwife. Only after he was delivered and I wrapped him snugly in the wrap I brought for my new babe, did we gaze at him ever long whispering what we had been told. We marveled that those words were now wrapped in this tiny bit of flesh we held.

We wondered together how long before others around would know who our babe really was. That question was answered before we could even start back home. A group of shepherds arrived at our stable wanting to see our babe. Joseph, first skeptical of allowing them in our tiny space, quickly learned of angels visiting them announcing Jesus' birth. We heard once again from the mouths of shepherds now, that our babe Jesus was Savior, Christ the Lord.

At eight days we followed tradition again and Jesus was circumcised. At one month and a half we traveled the short distance to Jerusalem to present Jesus to God in the temple. Often when we were experiencing ordinary life, Joseph at his carpentry work and I with our small household, an event would astound us, shaking us to our very souls.

Our temple experience was just that. The old priest Simeon took our babe and praised God declaring the true identity of our son. Then he spoke directly to me.

"This child is destined to cause the falling and rising of many in Israel, and to be a sign that will be spoken against, so that the thoughts of many hearts will be revealed. And a sword will pierce your own soul too"(Lk. 2: 34-35).

Anna, the aged and beloved prophetess, approached us as well, praising God that she could lay eyes on her Messiah, for whom she had prayed for decades.

A sword would pierce my soul? I did not understand Simeon's words. I remembered the day less than a year before when I skipped to the well, lighthearted. Looking back, I have spent hours pondering, wondering at words I have heard. Words of promise and words that declared my soul would be pierced tumbled together. Blessings and promise accompanied by piercing pain? Our trip back to Bethlehem was uneventful. I cradled my son in my arms, grateful for a healthy son, my husband, and ordinary days ahead in our small home.

One ordinary afternoon, my friend rushed into our small home. "You have visitors on the way! Several! Wealthy!" Her words tumbled out breathlessly.

"Please get Joseph," I said. Hurriedly I swept our tiny courtyard. Yes, I had grain and could make extra loaves quickly. We had only dried figs and raisins. Our meager offerings of hospitality would be given willingly. Thankfully, Joseph arrived just moments before one of the strangest events one could imagine.

Richly dressed men arrived on camels. Their entourage was too great to enter our tiny courtyard. Neighbors offered to bring water for their camels in the street. Children peeked out from behind their mothers' cloaks, wide-eyed at the luxurious tassels on the camels' saddles. We welcomed these men into our tiny home. They explained how they studied the stars for wisdom. A great and unique star had appeared and hovered over Bethlehem on exactly the night our son was born.

While Joseph and I were amazed at their visit, we were not surprised by what they revealed. They were told the star was the rising of the King of the Jews. They came to pay homage and present gifts. We showed them our son, ordinary in appearance. Yet they marveled and confirmed they were seeing the King of the Jews. They bowed to our son declaring words of honor and homage to him. They opened treasure chests unlike anything we had ever seen. As they spread out their gifts, Joseph and I bowed in thanksgiving. Gold, frankincense, and myrrh. These would be the only earthly treasures our son would ever have.

We politely inquired about their trip to find us. They had traveled through Jerusalem inquiring where we lived. They clearly stated they wanted to visit the next King of the Jews. Herod would have caught wind of that quickly. He should have known prophecy to know where the Messiah would be born. He did not, and had to assemble his leaders. The chief priests and scribes of the people informed them of our town. The wise men observed again the star they saw on the night of our son's birth and pressed on. We later learned Herod was intent that no king of the Jews should exist except who he declared, and who his compromised, if not evil, leaders approved as well.

We knew the evil heart of Herod. Our visitors spent the night sleeping in our courtyard. Thankfully, neighbors shared from their grain and fruit. We were able to send them on their way with olives, dates, and figs for their journey. Before they left, they discretely told us that in a dream the night before, they were told to not do Herod's bidding. He had instructed them to return and tell him where the one to be King of the Jews resided. They were told in the dream to return a different way, not honoring King Herod's request.

Our lives returned to normal for a short while. Each night Joseph and I lay down, now as husband and wife, Jesus on a tiny mat near us.

Joseph was gently shaking me! In the black of night he whispered hoarsely that we had to leave immediately. I lit a tiny lamp so we could gather what little we could carry on our one donkey. "Hurry, for our son's sake," was all I needed to hear. We left Bethlehem before daybreak having said goodbye to no one. Thankfully, we passed no one we knew that first day on the rugged path south. At next sunrise we looked down on the land of the Philistines. Joseph said little in the first two days of our journey. His countenance was troubled. I waited. He would speak in his own time. When he did, I felt a sword pierce my soul for the first time.

The Lord had appeared to him in a dream with a message of terror. King Herod intended to find our Jesus and kill him. We were to leave not only Bethlehem, but our country. Egypt would be our home until the Lord directed otherwise.

King Herod was cruel beyond measure. We knew this. He would strike. And he did. Word traveled faster than we could. We were leaving Gaza to face the heat of the desert when we heard the dreaded news. King Herod had required that all the boys under age two in our town and surrounding area be slaughtered.

I remembered the faces of my childhood friends at the well, mothers with young boys now. Pictures raced through my mind of King Herod's soldiers on horses descending on our quiet village, snatching babes and toddlers from their mothers' arms, plunging their swords into their small chests. Pillaging homes and courtyards, pulling small children that had been hidden. Killing, killing, killing. It was as if I heard the wails of my friends and relatives weeping for their children. All because of my son. My soul could hardly bear the pain.

The next two days in the desert were hot beyond imagination. Sand dunes glowing like the sun, one flowing into the next, wind flinging stinging sand into our faces. When we arrived at the Nile River my heart felt like a seared hot stone. I remembered again the visit of the beautiful creature. I pondered again his reassuring words. Jesus, our Messiah. I must focus simply on being his mother.

Thankfully, Egypt would not be our permanent home. I was grateful when Joseph was again visited in a dream. We could return to our country, but not through Bethlehem. For the sake of our son, we settled in Nazareth.

———

Mary, no doubt, watched her young son grow. Brothers and sisters came. But Jesus was unique. Mary pondered those first words of the angel, the words of Elizabeth and Simeon. She never doubted those words. But she often wondered again about the question she had first asked that angel. "How can this be?"

———

How can my eldest, racing with his siblings, growing in responsibility in helping me, be the Messiah? He often must find his younger brothers and bring them home. He gathers wood for our fires. Joseph is now training him in carpentry. So ordinary. The impossible miracle of my son's conception now seems small compared to how this boy becoming man could be our Messiah. The daily demands of our growing household crowded out my moments of contemplation.

Festival time came. I loved this time to go with the throng of family and friends to Jerusalem. Freed from the daily responsibilities, it was a time of celebration. Being with other women and their families rekindled our ties of friendship. Too soon it was time to return home. Jesus, now twelve, was old enough to walk with the men. My friends and I chatted with our young children beside us. My youngest, our fourth son, lay close on my back in my cloak.

At the end of the first day of traveling, our men joined us. We regrouped as families for our evening meal. Jesus was missing! Joseph thought he was with me, helping with his younger brothers. Distraught, we entrusted our children to friends and returned to search for Jesus. He was not at any of the expected and familiar places. Our relatives who lived there had not seen him. Our fears grew. Had Archelaus, Herod's son who now ruled, kidnapped him?

On the third day, in desperation we visited the temple. Our son! Sitting with the teachers, not simply listening, but questioning. We approached with frustration, crowding out the awe of what we were seeing and hearing.

It was I who spoke: "Child, why have you treated us like this? Look, your father and I have been searching for you in great anxiety."

Jesus was now the height of his father. He respectfully, yet with assurance in his voice, declared, "Why were you searching for me? Did you not know that I must be in my Father's house?"

What parent would understand such words from a twelve-year-old son? I saw Joseph's look of frustration change to resigned recognition. We both knew the truth of Jesus' words, yet that reality had not struck us before so profoundly. Thankfully he returned with us, obeying us as he always had.

I added those words of my son to the many I continued to ponder. What was next for our Messiah? My son Jesus?

At the age of twelve Jesus was debating with the Scribes in the temple. His wisdom was beginning to show that he was like no other. Wise beyond his age, bold beyond his stature as a carpenter's son. I watched, and tried to imagine what was ahead. I had listened to the words of the Torah and the prophets. I remembered references to the Messiah. I had pondered the wonderful promises before. Now I began to ponder those that were troubling.

I concluded that simply trusting my Lord for each ordinary day was the best I could do.

JESUS AS AN ADULT AND HIS CRUCIFIXION

By the time Jesus reached manhood, my husband had died. Jesus, being a good son, was a carpenter and supported me and his younger siblings. He trained my sons well in the trade. But the time came when his Heavenly Father's call was greater. He spent more time away from home. His brothers provided for me with their carpentry skills. I eagerly listened when people spoke of him. I knew he had traveled to Bethany. Word came that his cousin John baptized him in the river Jordan. John urged his followers to follow Jesus instead of himself, declaring Jesus' true identity. My son was gathering others, friends that seemed closer than his brothers. While I wished my children embraced my eldest, they did not. Mothers cannot create bonds between siblings. I knew this. Yet what mother ever relinquishes her dream of her children embracing each other, peace and unity in the family?

Yet, he came to my side when I asked. One such occasion was a wedding in nearby Cana. Being a widow, it was expected that my eldest son accompany me to the celebration. I was humbly proud to have Jesus at my side. To the dismay of our hosts, they ran out of wine. I knew Jesus could solve this in ways impossible to others. When I brought that to my son's attention, he reminded me his "time had not come." Yet, I told a servant to do whatever Jesus told him to do. I somehow sensed Jesus would act.

He did in a most amazing way. There were six large jars, each of which could hold twenty or thirty gallons of water. Jesus told the servants to fill them to the top. In a flurry of activity they did so. Looking expectantly to this unusual man, they listened. "Draw some out and take it to the chief steward to taste." They obeyed; amazed it was no longer water, but more than 150 gallons of wine. The chief steward pronounced it superb. He questioned the bridegroom as to why he saved the best wine for last. It should have been served first while the guests could truly savor it. The servants watched in amazement. They were the first to recognize Jesus' first miracle. They motioned the chief steward to them. "He told us to fill the jars! It was water! We swear it!" Their words tumbled on top of each other, each confirming what seemed an impossible thing. The bridegroom would be told later. His disciples savored the improved wine, remembering Jesus talking to the servants. They would later recall this as his first miracle. His glory was first revealed at a wedding prompted by a comment from his mother.

My son began teaching about his true Father, healing, blessing, feeding, doing miracles. The Pharisees were jealous. The Sadducees were angry. Common folks were curious and followed him for food and healing. I watched. I listened as neighbors from our home town discredited him. I was concerned. How would he react to the constant criticism? I was concerned for his health and fatigued state as he was constantly followed and criticized. Not even his disciples could keep the crowds from him. Could he not be granted a time of relief? He miraculously fed thousands at different times. He moved to Capernaum, which was a bustling cross roads of our country. Merchants passed through bringing spices from the East. The Sea of Galilee provided a vigorous fishing industry. He needed to travel little to be in the midst of crowds and talking to throngs of people who then spread out retelling his miracles and all they saw and experienced.

He reminded the crowds that true family were those who believed in his Heavenly Father, a concept many could not or would not embrace. His younger brothers did not take kindly to this, especially after we reached out to him in our concern. We heard he was thin and exhausted. We knew the crowds pressed him relentlessly. Surely his brothers and I could convince him to rest, take a time of refreshment from the life he seemed compelled to live. Arriving where he stayed in Capernaum, the crowds around were too thick for us to move through. When he heard his family was outside wishing to see him, he again stated that his true family were those who followed him.

I saw the disapproval in Jesus' brothers' eyes as we made our way home. Had they not taken on the responsibility for my care, something that was my eldest son's responsibility? Were they not burdened by the threats on his life? They did not embrace him as the Messiah. Yet he was their brother.

As the accolades for his miracles became louder, so did the death threats. Jewish leaders wanted this threat to their power to go away. The Romans feared Jesus might gain too much popularity. I watched. I remembered.

One night as I pondered, it seemed as though every fear and every disappointment weighed on me beyond my ability to bear it. I remembered the looks of hatred in the faces of the Pharisees and Sadducees when Jesus spoke in the synagogues. I remembered Roman soldiers skirting the crowds around him. They found him revolting. A poor Jew claiming to be the Messiah. I sensed they would kill him in an instant, brutally if possible, like they would swat a fly after pulling off its legs. And then Nazareth, our home through his childhood, my friends and relatives, they rejected him as well.

It was reported to me that in our synagogue, after Jesus spoke, the leaders and the entire crowd shoved and chased him to the brow of a hill to throw him to his death. Our town, my son! I felt a sword piercing my soul—again.

The months took flight. I continued to hear of Jesus' miracles, parables he told to illustrate truths. He healed the sick, visited sinners, conversed with women, blessed and held children. Many could not accept that a King of the Jews, their Messiah, would engage in such outrageous behavior.

I was not surprised. Jesus, my son and my Savior, would do this.

I pored over words of prophecy I had been taught since my childhood. Yes, a cruel death of our Messiah was told. I could not help but study those words more carefully. My mind rebelled, tempting me to deny those truths. My mother's heart could not refute prophecy. Would that I could spare my Jesus what those words said were ahead.

Passover time came bringing a sense of foreboding. As had become my habit after Joseph's death, I went to Jerusalem to stay with relatives. We would celebrate together. Just as in my home town, people who knew me approached me with word of Jesus. It seemed no one could get enough of scrutinizing and reporting everything he did. Some women seemed to delight in telling me spiteful questions continually hurled at him with insults. I learned to discern their intent and listen lightly, instead savoring the reports of healing and comfort.

One of the most precious reports was of a lengthy conversation one woman reported they had at a well. She reported that he knew everything about her, ample reason to shun her. Yet he listened, already knowing what she spoke. She revealed her amazement at his freeing her from the guilt of her past life. His forgiveness and gift of comfort changed her forever. She became a herald in her own town that Jesus, my son, was not only the Messiah, but her Messiah!

I heard of the Passover meal he shared with his followers. Word came he was preparing them for his death, their life without him. I was thankful to hear he left the city every night to sleep on the Mount of Olives. I felt he was safer there. Yet on this night, I could not sleep. My mind replayed my life with him from the moment of birth through his childhood into adulthood. First I remembered only good and ordinary days. Days of teaching him, seeing him work beside Joseph, seeing him race with his brothers through the village. I was grateful to have these memories to ponder. And then those not so ordinary days replayed in my mind. The shepherds' and kings' visits. His wisdom in the temple at age twelve. His unusual obedience to Joseph and me. And then his loyalty to the calling of his Heavenly Father. I wished the night would last forever. Each of these memories would be my treasure forever.

The next day came. Though my mind knew it would come, I pushed back thinking of it. Yet prophecy was truth. Word came of the arrest of my Jesus. He had been taken to the high priest's house. I knew he would suffer being held by the temple police. How many times had they hungered to kill him? I would fast and pray continually for him. I heard he was taken before the council. They decided to take him to Pilate for trial. Pilate, being the political figure he was, sent him to Herod. The pretense was that Jesus was of Galilee and therefore under Herod's jurisdiction.

The truth was that Pilate and Herod were enemies and Pilate would wish for Herod to declare a decision that would incite rioting rather than having to do it himself.

Strange, Herod sent him back only after his soldiers further abused my precious son. What followed would have been beyond belief, except that many reported the same. Pilate released one guilty of insurrection and murder—released him instead of Jesus, and turned my son over to the chief priests and leaders to execute him by crucifixion.

I could no more prevent my feet from rushing to be at my son's side than I could stop the sun from rising. I rushed into the crowded streets. Knowing the custom of the one to be hung carrying his cross to the killing hill, I would find a place to glimpse his precious face. Throngs in the street blocked my every turn. Some were weeping. Some were cursing and shouting vile words of triumph. I realized I would not get to him through those crowds. I must get to that dreaded hill. I followed a circuitous route to the hill of Golgotha.

I arrived in time to see them lift his cross and drop it with a deadening thud into the hole. Even I would not have recognized him. But his eyes, those precious eyes, were his. Yes, our gazes met. His eyes held that same look of love as when he was a babe at my breast; he nursed and looked intently into my face. He was butchered and beaten beyond appearance as a human. But I would not look away. I watched each breath. I did not hear the crowd's jeers and taunts, but I heard and treasured each word Jesus spoke. Each hour seemed endless yet each moment priceless. I would never again experience the nearness of my son, my Jesus.

⸻

That awful time of my son's crucifixion was beyond belief. Being a human mother, having held him as he took his first breath, having stroked his soft cheek as he nursed, the pain in my body was beyond bearing. Seeing him, unrecognizable on that cross from torture, my arms ached to hold him, wipe the blood from his face, touch water on his lips, cradle his treasured body, no matter how broken, next to my heart. I could only look up, watch him struggling to push with his feet hammered through with spikes. But push up he must, so his diaphragm could suck in air for one more sentence.

"Near the cross of Jesus stood his mother, his mother's sister, Mary the wife of Clopas, and Mary Magdalene. When Jesus saw his mother there, and the disciple whom he loved standing nearby, he said to her, 'Woman, here is your son,' and to the disciple, 'Here is your mother.' From that time on, this disciple took her into his home"(Jn. 19: 25-27).

⸻

I knew the moment my son died. He decided that moment. He committed himself into the hands of his true Father. He was gone.

I watched as the Roman guards fulfilled their duty. Even in their brutality, they allowed us to follow our customs. They broke the legs of the others being crucified to hasten their deaths. It was evident that Jesus was already dead. One guard thrust his spear into my son's side. As my son's blood flowed, I felt that spear in my own side all the way through to my heart.

Those words would replay thousands of times in her ears. "Woman, here is your son," and to the disciple, "Here is your mother." Those words would never be forgotten, seared into her memory, her son's last words to her. Even dying, he provided for her. John, his dearest friend, would take care of his mother. Jesus knew best. His brothers did not believe him, John KNEW. Mary would be loved and treasured in John's household.

Quiet tumult followed the next day. Many of my son's followers hid fearing their Jewish brothers would kill them for insurrection. The Scribes and Pharisees were jubilant. They had preserved their pious leadership positions from this imposter. I stayed cloistered in my relative's home. I ate nothing, received only a few friends who simply sat beside me. I declined to see most. I simply waited. The story of my Jesus was not finished.

Jesus' friends, including Mary Magdalene, went to the tomb on Sunday morning to prepare his body with spices, as our tradition required. Some might have thought I would go. I could not. I would simply listen to their reports and wait. I made plans to move my few belongings into John's home.

What followed confounded many, frightened some, and simply confirmed what I knew. Jesus was not in the tomb. Not a day, sometimes an hour, passed that I did not hear some truths and some rumors. Jesus did appear to his disciples. He appeared to others who were open to his words. More than a month passed. I decided I would join his followers. I sensed another significant day approaching.

Forty days after his Resurrection, I joined the gathering of his followers. I feasted my eyes on him. He was different. I no longer saw him as first my son. He was now my Savior. He proved his power over death. I listened as he gave us instruction. We were to stay in Jerusalem until we received the Holy Spirit. And then I watched him go. He rose, gravity could not contain him, and the earth could not claim him. He was returning to his Father. I could only rejoice.

———

What followed? We are told little about Mary's days after Jesus' death. He appeared to his friends and many disciples. Mary might well have been in those gatherings, seen him, feasted her eyes on the fulfillment of every word she was promised.

It would also have been accepted if she were not in those groups hovering often in fear, behind closed doors after his crucifixion. Understandably, she could have secluded herself from the piercing glances of those who both loved her son and hated him.

We do know she was with his followers after Jesus returned to heaven, joining them in prayer. We know his brothers were there as well. Finally! They believed! Their brother was more than their brother. He was their Messiah.

Scripture has told us all we need to know about Jesus' mother. A tenacious woman, unlike any other, who knew Jesus in ways no other person would ever know him. Mary, not remembered as a widow, but as the mother of Jesus.

STUDY GUIDE
Lk. 1: 26-38; Mt. 1: 18-23, Lk. 2: 51-52; Mt. 13: 53-57; Mk. 6: 31; Mt. 12: 46-50; Jn. 19: 25-27; Acts 1: 12. Additional references: Lk. 2: 41-51; Jn. 2: 1-11; Mt. 12: 46-50; Mk. 3: 31-34; Lk. 8:21; Acts 1: 14,12: 12

Mary, the mother of Jesus, had tenacity like few others. Birthing Jesus as a teenager, she knew her assignment was like no other. He experienced conflict with brothers, criticism from religious counterparts, and adulthood defined by political chaos. In a sense, Mary was his first disciple. Consider that for the first three decades of Jesus' life, Mary loved, watched, and impacted his days, though I imagine his impact on her was greater. During his ministry years, she is often with his followers and when not, knowledgeable of his activities. More importantly, she was obedient to God's instructions and call on her life—the mark of a true disciple.

And then she watched him die the most dreaded, painful death possible. I'm sure Mary's pain was like no other mother's pain in all history. After all, there was no one like her son. She had no choice but to bear this awful pain alone. In another sense, paradoxically, her mother's grief was universal. Every mother whose child is torn from her by tragedy suffers with Mary.

But after his death, she met with his followers. Grief did not draw her into hibernation. She waited expectantly for God to work. And He did.

HIS BIRTH

In the sixth month of Elizabeth's pregnancy, God sent the angel Gabriel to Nazareth, a town in Galilee, to a virgin pledged to be married to a man named Joseph, a descendant of David. The virgin's name was Mary. The angel went to her and said, "Greetings, you who are highly favored! The Lord is with you." Mary was greatly troubled at his words and wondered what kind of greeting this might be. But the angel said to her, "Do not be afraid, Mary; you have found favor with God. You will conceive and give birth to a son, and you are to call him Jesus. He will be great and will be called the Son of the Most High. The Lord God will give him the throne of his father David, and he will reign over Jacob's descendants forever; his kingdom will never end."

"How will this be," Mary asked the angel, "since I am a virgin?"

The angel answered, "The Holy Spirit will come on you, and the power of the Most High will over-shadow you. So the holy one to be born will be called the Son of God. Even Elizabeth your relative is going to have a child in her old age, and she who was said to be unable to conceive is in her sixth month. For no

word from God will ever fail." "I am the Lord's servant," Mary answered. "May your word to me be
fulfilled." Then the angel left her (Lk. 1: 26).

This is how the birth of Jesus the Messiah came
about: His mother Mary was pledged to be married
to Joseph, but before they came together, she was
found to be pregnant through the Holy Spirit.
Because Joseph her husband was faithful to the law,
and yet did not want to expose her to public disgrace,
he had in mind to divorce her quietly. But after he
had considered this, an angel of the Lord appeared
to him in a dream and said, "Joseph son of David,
do not be afraid to take Mary home as your wife,
because what is conceived in her is from the Holy
Spirit. She will give birth to a son, and you are to give
him the name Jesus, because he will save his people
from their sins."

All this took place to fulfill what the Lord had said
through the prophet: "The virgin will conceive and give
birth to a son, and they will call him Immanuel"(which
means God with us) [Mt. 1: 18].

HIS CHILDHOOD

Then he went down to Nazareth with them and was
obedient to them. But his mother treasured all these

things in her heart. And Jesus grew in wisdom and stature, and in favor with God and man (Lk. 2: 51).

HIS MINISTRY

When Jesus had finished these parables, he moved on from there. Coming to his hometown, he began teaching the people in their synagogue, and they were amazed. "Where did this man get this wisdom and these miraculous powers?" they asked. "Isn't this the carpenter's son? Isn't his mother's name Mary, and aren't his brothers James, Joseph, Simon and Judas? Aren't all his sisters with us? Where then did this man get all these things?" And they took offense at him. But Jesus said to them, "A prophet is not without honor except in his own town and in his own home"(Mt. 13: 53).

"Isn't this the carpenter? Isn't this Mary's son and the brother of James, Joseph, Judas and Simon? Aren't his sisters here with us?" And they took offense at him (Mk. 6: 3).

While Jesus was still talking to the crowd, his mother and brothers stood outside, wanting to speak to him. Someone told him, "Your mother and brothers are standing outside, wanting to speak to you."

He replied to him, "Who is my mother, and who are my brothers?" Pointing to his disciples, he said, "Here are my mother and my brothers. For whoever does the will of my Father in heaven is my brother and sister and mother"(Mt. 12: 46-50).

HIS DEATH

Near the cross of Jesus stood his mother, his mother's sister, Mary the wife of Clopas, and Mary Magdalene. When Jesus saw his mother there, and the disciple whom he loved standing nearby, he said to her, "Woman, here is your son," and to the disciple, "Here is your mother." From that time on, this disciple took her into his home" (Jn. 19: 25-27).

Then the apostles returned to Jerusalem from the hill called the Mount of Olives, a Sabbath day's walk from the city. They all joined together constantly in prayer, along with the women and Mary the mother of Jesus, and with his brothers (Acts 1: 12).

BIRTH AND CHILDHOOD

1. What uniquely prepared Mary to be the mother of Jesus?
2. What uniquely prepared Joseph to be Jesus' earthly father?

3. If you are a parent, what lessons can you learn
   from Mary? From Joseph?

THINKING IT OVER

Mary's need for wisdom was great in every season. From the time the angel told her she would birth Jesus, her challenges were extreme. Her need for wisdom was great. Scripture assures us God will supply this need.

> If any of you is lacking in wisdom, ask God, who gives
> to all generously and ungrudgingly, and it will be given
> you (James 1: 5 NSRV).

———

On our need for wisdom:

> "For my thoughts are not your thoughts,
> neither are your ways my ways,"
> declares the LORD.
> As the heavens are higher than the earth,
> so are my ways higher than your ways
> and my thoughts than your thoughts.
> As the rain and the snow
> come down from heaven,
> and do not return to it
> without watering the earth
> and making it bud and flourish,
> so that it yields seed for the sower and bread for the eater,

so is my word that goes out from my mouth:
It will not return to me empty,
but will accomplish what I desire
and achieve the purpose for which I sent it (Is. 55:
8-11).

———

The Sovereign Lord is my strength;
he makes my feet like the feet of a deer,
he enables me to tread on the heights (Hab. 3: 19).

PERSONAL APPLICATION

1. Ask God to give you the gift of simple faith to trust when you don't understand.
2. What steps of obedience can you take to show God the reality of your trust?
3. If you are a parent, consider that each of us must relinquish each child (young or adult) to God.
4. Consider that God is better able to guide your child (children) and loves them more than you do or can.

ADULTHOOD AND DEATH

1. How did Mary demonstrate her human, motherly instincts when Jesus was an adult?
2. What challenges do mothers face whose children choose different belief systems?

3. What example does Mary set as the mother of
   Jesus during his adulthood and after his Resurrection?

PERSONAL APPLICATION

1. As you consider Mary's story, what stands out to
   you in her character?
2. Why were these character traits important given
   her life assignment?
3. What challenges would she face in her steps of
   obedience?

NINE

INDUSTRIOUS
Abigail, the Widow of Nabal, then Bride of David

I Samuel 25: 2-42

Packing again. Maon was home, but her husband's property was in Carmel. She loved home, peace, the comforts of her friends in Maon, the community. But she married Nabal, and his property was in Carmel. It was expected that she accompany him at sheep shearing time.

Abigail directed her workers and servants to load needed food supplies for their time in Carmel and all the household utensils and housing needs; sleeping mats, and added tents for sheep shearing time in Carmel. They responded quickly with eyes of respect. Without Abigail's oversight, things would go wrong. Nabal would curse them or worse. They would arrive lacking what they needed. Nabal was lucky to have Abigail. They all knew it.

Abigail left her household packing and walked to the tent where preparations were being made for packing shearing supplies. The hot wind blew dust in her face, but went unnoticed, so focused was she on the myriad details of the trip. In the tent, preparations were being made for the shearing burdens the donkeys would carry. Coarse language ceased as the men saw her coming.

"Greetings, Abigail. Our preparations are going well," the foreman, Joash, said with respect.

"Remember that Nabal expects a great celebration after shearing," Abigail said. "Prepare donkeys to carry wine, barley, and all we need to prepare for the gathering."

Joash nodded in acknowledgment. How many times had Abigail's oversight kept him from incurring Nabal's wrath, usually for something he had forgotten to oversee? He knew they would incur the harshest wrath if they ran out of wine. While Nabal's men at the celebration would consume much, Nabal had an endless appetite, unquenchable on more days than sheep shearing times.

Joash would add more donkeys for extra food. He watched Abigail with admiration as she left. Why should ill-tempered, foolish Nabal be blessed with one of such beauty and wisdom? Her industry and intelligence meant there would be figs, raisins, and grain for bread-making. Work and celebrations at Carmel would go well because of Abigail.

Abigail made one last stop to bid her friend goodbye. How often had Ana told her of God's work among their people and taught her God's ways. Her last bit of news was that the young valiant warrior, David, had been anointed king of their nation. But, King Saul not only refused to give up his position, but had threatened David's life. Ana and Abigail knelt and prayed together that Yahweh would guide and protect them all. Abigail reluctantly hurried off with much left to do.

Thankfully the trip from Maon to Carmel was short, almost pleasant, a pause in responsibilities, a time to feel almost free of the load she constantly carried. Her mind returned to the dilemma of their king. Word traveled through the country that David had been anointed king by Samuel, their revered prophet. Could it be true that Saul had changed so completely from his early years as king? He was initially reluctant, he continued even plowing his own fields as a new king, humble indeed. And then word spread of his jealousy of David's success above his on the battlefields. Could he really have attempted to murder his greatest warrior, one he took into his home almost as a son? Abigail looked across the barren hills leaving Maon. What would Yahweh do? Surely her God would not allow chaos to continue among His chosen people. A hot, harsh wind whipped her shawl about her face. She pulled her head wrap down and grasped it under her chin. She would hear little on this subject in Carmel. She sighed with relief. At least the demands of sheep shearing time and celebrating would crowd out all thoughts of the possible chaos in her country.

The sheep shearing was going well, very well. Of all that could be said against Nabal's character, he was successful in oversight of his vast herds of sheep—three thousand, and one thousand goats. His expert breeding practices, knowledge of where they should graze, and getting the most from each animal was his strength. Perhaps his only characteristic greater than his business acumen was his pride.

Abigail set up their nomadic home. Oversight of food needs for hundreds of workers, soothing relationships behind Nabal's constant irritations, Abigail sensed her God with her all the time.

Her routine was disrupted. One of Nabal's young men rushed into her tent. He spilled the story of David's request for gifts of food from Nabal for the protection his men gave Nabal's herdsmen and flocks while in the wilderness; a reasonable request. "David sent messengers from the wilderness to give our master his greetings, but he hurled insults at them. Yet these men were very good to us. They did not mistreat us, and the whole time we were out in the fields near them nothing was missing. Night and day they were a wall around us the whole time we were herding our sheep near them. Now think it over and see what you can do, because disaster is hanging over our master and his whole household. He is such a wicked man that no one can talk to him" (I Sam. 25: 14-17).

Quick of action, and quicker of thought, Abigail realized her brutish husband had just signed a death warrant for every male on Nabal's team including himself. She knew she must act quickly. The anointed young King David was already renowned as a warrior. Thankfully, she knew that to a person, every one in the camp would follow her instruction. Her own strength, endurance, and respected leadership formed her firm foundation for such a time as this.

Abigail acted quickly. She took two hundred loaves of bread, two skins of wine, five dressed sheep, five seahs[a] of roasted grain, a hundred cakes of raisins and two hundred cakes of pressed figs, and loaded them on donkeys. Then she told her servants, "Go on ahead; I'll follow you." But she did not tell her husband Nabal (I Sam. 25: 18-19).

As her entourage entered a ravine, David and his men descended on her. Her servants watched in awe as their mistress did something they had never seen her do. She got off her donkey, approached David, and fell at his feet, face to the ground. They heard their mistress speak to this king with respect, with insight beyond common sense, and with prophetic accuracy.

Abigail entreated the enraged David, accurately describing Nabal's error, and appealed to what Abigail knew to be David's strength. His sure knowledge that he was the anointed king of Israel carried the accompanying obligation not to heedlessly spill blood.

> Please forgive your servant's presumption. The Lord your God will certainly make a lasting dynasty for my lord, because you fight the Lord's battles, and no wrongdoing will be found in you as long as you live. Even though someone is pursuing you to take your life, the life of my lord will be bound securely in the bundle of the living by the Lord your God, but the lives of your enemies he will hurl away as from the pocket of a sling. When the Lord has fulfilled for my lord every good thing he promised concerning him and has appointed him ruler over Israel, my lord will not have on his conscience the staggering burden of needless bloodshed or of having avenged himself. And when the Lord your God has brought my lord success, remember your servant (I Sam. 25: 28-31).

David accepted Abigail's gifts of food and wine. He praised her for her good judgment, and affirmed that, indeed, he had been intent on murdering Nabal and his men. He took note that she referenced the effectiveness of a slingshot. This strange and beautiful woman must have known of his first victory over the giant, Goliath. He would not forget Abigail.

The jostling ride on her donkey back home was not nearly as shaking as her competing emotions. Saving her family, men, and servants from death should have brought joy. But her heart was heavy. Back to life with a surly man, a fool, with whom life was never peaceful.

She slipped quietly into her bed, avoiding telling her husband about such a significant day. As he reveled and drank, she rested her tired head on her mat, wishing for a man she could love and depend on, wishing for a conversation with one who would understand and embrace God as she did. Tomorrow would bring its own challenges, not the least of which would be to tell Nabal what she'd done. How she wanted the wish she had for David's life, "the life of my lord will be bound securely in the bundle of the living by the Lord your God." How she prayed that would be true in her own life.

Fatigue won out and she slept dreaming of what it would be like to experience a life safe "in the bundle of the living by the Lord my God."

Though the morning light was welcome, her first task of the day was not.

Nabal did not waken until noon. I watched him stumble toward the loaves I had just spread with cheese. I must tell him now, I thought. Yes, his eyes were red, but he was sober. I took a deep breath and recounted our gifts to David, my words, and part of my plea. I simply told him that David was satisfied and would not be attacking our camp. His hand jerked to his chest. It was as if his heart failed him. He became like a stone. It was as if the rigors of death had overtaken him. Yet he breathed. I summoned his slaves to move him to comfort. For ten days he did not move except for breathing. Surely his youth and his life of physical exertion would win out. His eyes would open, he would move a finger, tilt his head. After ten days, he died.

The word spread quickly. David praised God for sparing him bold, but wrong revenge. He acted quickly. He sent word to Abigail asking her to become his wife. Again, her servants watched as their mistress who led them assumed the position of a servant, bowed her face to the ground, and said, "I am your servant and am ready to serve you and wash the feet of my lord's servants." Abigail quickly got on a donkey and, attended by her five female servants, went with David's messengers and became his wife.

There is little mention of Abigail as David's wife. We know it was complicated. She and another of David's wives were captured, but he safely got them back unharmed by the enemy who took them. She bore at least one son. David's life was anything but peace filled. He acquired more wives and concubines. Being the wife of a warrior meant security was not a part of "being bound securely in the bundle of the living by the Lord your God."

Abigail made the choice within days of becoming a widow to accept David's offer of marriage. Some believe Solomon, David's son who inherited his throne, wrote a proverb about her. Some believed he spoke of his mother Bathsheba. But most believed Proverbs 31, which praises the ideal wife, was written from Solomon's knowledge of Abigail.

STUDY GUIDE
I SAMUEL 25: 2-42

Widows often experience extreme change. Abigail was no exception. Scripture tells us she was intelligent and beautiful, and her husband was rich—extremely rich. A life we would all envy, right? Wrong! Her wealthy husband, Nabal, was surly, mean, and became drunk on occasion. The source of his wealth meant they lived a lifestyle of the nomad.

In this marriage her godly, wise character was on display. Those who worked for Nabal reported to Abigail, obeyed and supported her. She knew God's will and God's ways. She was willing to risk her life for the honor of His name.

The black covering of widowhood came unexpectedly. It lasted a very short time. No doubt, Abigail grieved little, understandably. Her story is one of the most unique remarriage stories in Scripture.

A certain man in Maon, who had property there at Carmel, was very wealthy. He had a thousand goats and three thousand sheep, which he was shearing in Carmel. His name was Nabal and his wife's name was

Abigail. She was an intelligent and beautiful woman, but her husband was surly and mean in his dealings— he was a Calebite (I Sam. 25: 2-3).

———

When Abigail saw David, she quickly got off her donkey and bowed down before David with her face to the ground. She fell at his feet and said: "Pardon your servant, my lord, and let me speak to you; hear what your servant has to say. Please pay no attention, my lord, to that wicked man Nabal. He is just like his name—his name means Fool, and folly goes with him. And as for me, your servant, I did not see the men my lord sent. And now, my lord, as surely as the Lord your God lives and as you live, since the Lord has kept you from bloodshed and from avenging yourself with your own hands, may your enemies and all who are intent on harming my lord be like Nabal. And let this gift, which your servant has brought to my lord, be given to the men who follow you" (I Sam. 25: 23-27).

———

When David heard that Nabal was dead, he said, "Praise be to the Lord, who has upheld my cause against Nabal for treating me with contempt. He has kept his servant from doing wrong and has brought Nabal's wrongdoing down on his own head."

Then David sent word to Abigail, asking her to become his wife. His servants went to Carmel and said to Abigail, "David has sent us to you to take you to become his wife."

She bowed down with her face to the ground and said, "I am your servant and am ready to serve you and wash the feet of my lord's servants." Abigail quickly got on a donkey and, attended by her five female servants, went with David's messengers and became his wife (I Sam. 25: 39-42).

STUDY QUESTIONS

1. Consider what Abigail might have thought disadvantages in her marriage to Nabal that God used for His glory. List them.
2. Consider what you learned during marriage, even what you considered hard, that God might use in your new life as a single woman. List them.
3. How does the quality of one's marriage affect one's grieving process? Remember, don't compare.
4. What specific qualities and knowledge from Abigail's past enabled her to speak to David?

THINKING IT OVER

Abigail's knowledge of God's work among her people proved to be important, useful, and impactful at a strategic time in her life. We have the great treasure of having God's written Word to guide us. Time spent in His Word gives us great insights into our daily lives.

> Do your best to present yourself to God as one approved, a worker who does not need to be ashamed and who correctly handles the word of truth (II Tm. 2: 15).

> …so is my word that goes out from my mouth: It will not return to me empty, but will accomplish what I desire and achieve the purpose for which I sent it (Is. 55: 11).

We can know His priorities, His guidelines for living, and His heart for us.

Abigail's behavior reflected that her greatest loyalty was to God and secondly to Nabal. Her actions benefited David and Nabal. Her actions preserved David's reputation and kept Nabal from being killed by David. God had an outcome Abigail did not see in the moment. She acted on what she knew.

PERSONAL APPLICATION

1. Accept the differences in every person's grieving process. Remember, no one knows the details of another person's marriage.
2. Give yourself time to grieve on whatever time table that may be.

3. Step up to new opportunities and challenges during your grieving process.
4. Consider that stepping into new challenges and opportunities might strengthen you through your grieving process.

TEN

RISK-TAKER
Tamar, Twice Widowed and Childless

Genesis 38

Tamar leaned heavily into God and her understanding of His provision for family—no matter what. It's difficult for us to understand today the legacy of lineage and land ownership of that day. Yet, God sanctioned it.

Life and death seemed to cruelly stop Tamar at each transition of her life. She neither shrank from nor succumbed to circumstances. She became a risk taker. She is called a seducer and whore, but seldom referred to as a widow. History has treated her unkindly. Yet Judah declared her "more righteous than I." In fact, more accurate translations state, "She is righteous, not I." She risked death by burning in order to follow God's provision for widows. Her action also preserved Judah's legacy. At the time of her most noted action, Judah had no grandsons. Why does her legacy matter? Her son is in the lineage of Jesus.

I was once pretty. Named for the stately, ornamental tamarisk tree, my family was pleased, maybe even proud of me. And I lived up to my name. We were Canaanites, entrenched in our ways, our beliefs in our gods. Yes, we were clan-like, we looked out for each other. When our gods frowned, we offered an infant sacrifice. Our gods smiled again. One of our clan, Hirah, welcomed an outsider, Judah, into our midst. He married one of us, Shuah, and settled here and became prosperous. Shuah and my mother were friends. As Judah's sons were born, he did not offer one to our gods. By our customs, he should have offered his firstborn by fire to Baal. Strange. I would have had an older brother. But as an infant he was tossed into the burning stomach oven of Baal, so our family would prosper. We expected that prosperity would be denied Judah as he did not honor this custom. Not so. He prospered. My father told me this when I was young.

Always a curious one, I listened and learned. Judah's family worshipped a different God. They had no temple prostitutes. I was intrigued and learned all I could. Was it rumor or truth that this man Judah and his family were not to live with our people? Probably rumor. After all, he married one of us. Shuah, whose name meant wealth, came from a prosperous family. Hirah was known to be a loyal Canaanite, a respected leader in our area. He and Judah were more than men who worked together, they were friends. Hirah's approval meant we could trust Judah and his household. Shuah would ensure that their offspring followed our customs, with the exception of sacrificing their first son, Er. Judah's custom must have prevailed as all of her sons lived.

My childhood days were simple. Laughing with other girls, deciding what fabrics and colors we liked, fetching water. Gradually my mother trained me in household skills I would need later.

I had hardly entered my teen years when I noticed that men gazed at me a little too long. I was unafraid. My father was my protector. I knew he would decide on my husband, a good man for sure. I also knew that in our clan, sons were important. Land rights were passed from generation to generation. And with the land came responsibility to care for the women of the family, including widows. I thought little of this. But my mother and aunts made sure all of us as cousins and daughters knew these practices even though they seemed unimportant at the time. I barely listened as they explained the expected tradition that if one's husband died, his brother was to become the widow's husband and produce sons. If no son was left, it was expected that the widow's father-in-law would produce sons in her. I assumed Judah's beliefs were the same. After all, he married one of us. It seemed there were few differences between their people and our people. Compromise and accommodation were options.

Our families celebrated together at harvest time. My friends and I took advantage of the time to glance at the boys and young men. Judah's two older sons, Er and Oman, were of interest, but were not our people. Celebrations meant tables of food: raisins, figs, and wine in abundance. My favorite delicacy was dibs. This syrup made from grapes was a delicacy, served only at celebrations. Dipping my small loaf to take just a small portion, I looked up to see Er doing the same. I quickly looked down, but not before I noted that his eyes narrowed as they swept over my body.

Should I feel it a compliment to be noticed? Then why the sense of unrest with a twinge of fear that rose in me?

My brothers became friends with Er and Oman. They went out to examine flocks together. Judah's flocks seemed to prosper more than ours. While we had good stock, theirs produced more lambs. At shearing time, their wool was more desirable than ours. My brothers observed and learned from them. Our family prospered, although not as greatly as did theirs.

I overheard my brothers one night talk of their friends. Laughing, they said Er and Oman were even more successful with young women than their flocks. I wanted to ask them what that meant. I was sure they would laugh at me rather than answer.

Carefree little girl days disappeared into a season of preparing to be an adult woman. I sometimes helped care for babes in our clan. I learned to dry grapes for raisins and how to make my favorite grape honey. I learned to sort wool to use for different purposes: the finest to weave for fine robes, the more coarse for tunics. Thankfully my curiosity meant I listened and learned quickly.

Whatever my future might hold, I wanted not just my family to be proud, but our clan to be proud of Tamar.

To my great surprise and my father's as well, Judah asked for me to be the wife of his eldest son. "Er will be favored in inheritance," I overheard my mother say to my aunt. More important to my mind was the fact that we both favored grape honey.

Given what I had learned of their commitment to honoring land rights and inheritance though bearing sons, I knew my future was secure. Their beliefs mirrored ours in that matter. From what I had learned of the God they followed, they were good people. To marry Judah's eldest son meant we, Er and then our sons, would get a double portion of Judah's inheritance. My friends thought I was lucky. I stood tall.

Our marriage celebration was one of the grandest in our area. For days, every delicacy was prepared. Lambs were slaughtered. Fragrant grasses were brought to cover our compound floor. Wine skins filled with the best wine were brought to be poured into jugs during the great celebration. My mother and aunts created a gown for me that was beyond my imagination. Its brilliant colors lit my eyes and favored my honey brown complexion. The tight waist and flowing skirts—well, all said that I did honor to my name, the tall, stately, and beautiful tamarisk tree.

The day was a blur of greeting people, accepting gifts, and making sure Er and I greeted each person from his family and mine. Our ceremony was carefully planned by our fathers. Judah would offer a prayer to his God. Our priest would pledge our fidelity to our gods.

I trusted that the excitement of this day and the delight of being presented as Er's wife would be seared in my memory completely. This day would perhaps be the highlight of my life, second only to the moment I would give birth to our first son.

I did not even notice the hush among my family and our friends in our clan when Judah addressed his God. My mother later told me the same was true when my father petitioned our gods. Little did it matter to me. Er and I had knelt through them both.

The nearness of Er's body through the day flooded me with a strange desire. Tonight all would be consummated. I would enter all the satisfactions of being Er's wife.

Er was not the man I imagined him to be before marriage. Who would have imagined he could be so evil? He was abusive, cruel. He was gone for days at a time. When he returned, he had no interest in our marriage bed. I suspected the Canaanite temple prostitutes welcomed him, not because of his religious fervor and loyalty to Baal, but because he was handsome and would be wealthy. Surely Judah's God knew the heart of Er and Judah should have.

I came to expect and treasure the days he was gone. When he was tending to oversight of his flocks in other locations, or just gone for other reasons, my days were not filled with dread of the pain he would inflict on me at night. Solitude in our marriage bed was a treasure rather than lonely.

One night I heard him return. I pretended to sleep and turned to the wall, willing myself to be so small that he would not even notice my presence. He thudded down beside me. Gratefully I soon heard his soft snoring.

In the morning, I cautiously looked out from my coverlet hoping to slip from our bed unnoticed. He lay overly still and straight on his back, not his usual form. I looked closer. Was the morning light casting a gray shadow over him? I watched his chest. No movement. Was this a trick to draw me close so he could grab me? Some strange force drew me to put my face closer to his. His eyes were open and unmoving. I moved my hand quietly, close to his cheek. A shaft of light filtered through a window. I gasped and touched his still gray face. It was as though he had turned to cold stone.

I believe his God took his life.

I mourned openly, but not inside. The law of marriage of our people and his would still provide for me. His brother, Onan, was to take me as his wife. I would bear sons to continue Er's name and inheritance. I would be sustained by the family land. Life would go on. But I had a strong sense of dread for the future. Er and Onan had been inseparable friends. When Er was gone for days at a time, so was Onan.

Onan and I were married with no celebration. With only Judah, my father, Onan, and I present, a small sheepskin document declaring our union was prepared. It was signed by each of us. Judah and my father placed their imprint seal. I moved into Onan's quarters. Within days my fears were confirmed. I sensed quickly that his only concern was his lineage, his name, his family. He cared neither for his brother's name, his God's law or ours, or my well-being. He was evil as well, a betrayer, a hypocrite. He indulged his sexual desires on me, yet denied me a child, spilling his sperm. He used me for his pleasure. He was harsh, even brutal, and would whisper in my ear as we bedded together that I was responsible for his brother's death. Sometimes the glint in his eye caused my heart to shudder. Secretly I feared for my life.

Now I began to remember more vividly what my mother and aunts taught me. Land and birthright were to be divided between sons with a double portion to the firstborn. That meant Judah's inheritance would be divided in fourths. Two fourths to Er, one fourth to Onan, and one to Shelah. Onan's denying me a son meant his portion would now be larger. Judah's inheritance would be divided three ways. He would receive two portions and Shelah would receive one.

I saw the cunning in Onan's treatment of others in business and the mistreatment of his workers; surely Judah saw this as well. His treatment of me? Only the gods knew. But it was evident he neither honored any god nor loved me.

I tried to get acquainted with Onan's wife. She was polite, yet distant. A plain looking young woman, she seemed to resent me. Why should she? Onan spent most nights with her. Though their marriage celebration was shortly before Er's death and much less grand than ours had been, I was sure she would be with child before me.

I came to depend increasingly on the gods as I knew them, believing tenaciously that they had my best interests at heart. What might seem strange to some, God's law of marriage, I could see was for my protection and provision in our land and people. I knew the law and wondered, "What will become of Onan? What will become of me?" Surely both gods would punish Onan for his wickedness. Onan was ruthless. When he received the double inheritance that rightly belonged to Er, I knew without question he would not take care of me.

I concluded that Er's death was our gods protecting me. Surely the God of Judah, the One Who would not demand my infant in death, had a protective plan for me. What now? I never walked with Onan outside of our compounds, fearing he might dispose of me. I could tell no one my fear. They would not believe me and think me gone mad. Yet that foreboding lingered and grew.

One morning a neighbor rushed into my tiny courtyard. Grabbing my arm and pulling me to sit beside her, words tumbled out. She said in a hoarse whisper, "Onan is dead. He was as stone in his bed this morning. People are saying..." She did not need to say more. I knew some would believe I was the cursed cause of his death, even though he died in the bed of his first wife.

God had intervened, taking Onan's life. I was as sure of this as I was in the reality of discovering Er's stone-like body next to mine that fateful day. I was neither surprised, nor even sad. While still wearing my widow's veil, times of turmoil intensified. My people avoided me. My childhood friends now nursed their own children, cared for their husbands. At least, hiding behind my widow's veil, I could cloak my relief at no longer fearing for my safety, at having freedom from the abuse I suffered at the hands of my second husband.

Utterly alone, I determined to lean heavily on the gods. Judah had yet another son, much younger. Yet this grieving father looked at me differently now, with disdain. Hirah, his friend, looked at me as if I were not a person. Yet his eyes narrowed as they swept over my body. A bitter bile rose within me, threatening to turn my very soul sour with repulsion.

Would I forever be an object of lust? Would I ever experience tender love and be prized as a treasured, protected wife?

"Judah then said to his daughter-in-law Tamar, 'Live as a widow in your father's household until my son Shelah grows up'" (Gen. 38: 11 NRSV).

Judah asked me to wait until Shelah was of age when Judah would honor the law and provide yet another husband for me. Strange, the look in his eye. He would not look at me directly as he spoke. A strange foreboding gripped my soul. He was lying, a hypocrite like his son Onan.

Being back in my father's house was a disgrace. Judah should have supported me as a part of his family. I began to recognize a Judah that could not be trusted even to obey the laws he knew.

Time passed. I was not offered in marriage to Shelah. I was not surprised. I would gladly have remained single and worn the widow's garb the rest of my life. My father's household would sustain me. Simply, for sure, but I would survive. Yet, I sensed the strong sense of duty to bear a son. Certainty this was not out of loyalty to Judah; he had not earned it. Maybe it was to preserve my father's standing in our community. Struggling to sort my feelings, I succumbed to simply a sure knowledge that life ahead had more for me.

Imagine Tamar's predicament. A single woman, no rights in her father's house, denied God's plan for her provision by Judah who should have had her best interests at heart. At least he should have obeyed his law.

I wore my widow's veil well, drew water, made bread, tended to my father's house, and listened. Gradually, my sisters included me in their lives. They welcomed me into their homes to help with their children. I was even called to assist our midwife in delivering their babies. New life never ceased to amaze me. This tiny bit of humanity, totally dependent on his mother's breast, would grow to personhood.

My mother in law, Shuah, died. While she grieved deeply the death of her two oldest sons, she had doted on Shelah. Did she regret not offering her firstborn to Baal? Would Baal have then protected Onan from the minions of death that grabbed him? I was only a bit sorry for Judah but really could mourn no more. I went to their courtyard during the expected time of mourning. I was not surprised that few spoke to me. Judah avoided me as did Shelah and his betrothed wife-to-be. Even she eyed me with a bit of fear.

I pondered my options. I was now convinced Er and Onan had visited the temple prostitutes. Was that sanctioned by their father? Among our people, this was an act of religious fervor and a way to worship our gods. But I had learned that Judah's God forbade that. So Judah would never do that. Would he? My mind mulled these thoughts in the countless lonely hours of my life as a widow.

When Judah's mourning time was over, he and his friend Hirah were off to sheep shearing celebrations with his men in Timnah. All knew this would be a time of much drinking and carousing. Word traveled quickly of Judah's plan.

A plan began to emerge in my mind as well, one that would require extreme courage. I decided it would be better to throw myself on the mercies of their God, to honor His plans, rather than to trust Judah.

Risk! Courage! I would embrace both. But more than either, I believed God would act, and if not, I would still trust Him. My trust in the integrity of others, Judah and his clan, even the expected embrace of my own people after times of adversity, was shattered. God alone would be my strength. What good was it, believing it was His good wish to protect me, without being willing to act on His plan of provision?

I tucked what I needed into my tunic and headed for the road to Timnah. As I neared my destination, I slipped behind a grove of trees, shed my widow's garments, and hid them well. I wrapped myself in a garment I never intended to wear. I dressed as the temple prostitutes might—covering my face—which my sisters said was still beautiful. I chose the colors I remembered from my first wedding day. Donning the festive robe I went back to the roadside I knew they would travel. I waited. My heart pounded. I wanted no intimacy with any other man, ever, especially this Judah who could not be trusted. But God promised me a son. Committed to action, I would either be rewarded with life and children, or burned as a whore.

Judah's party approached. He noticed me and stopped. His band of friends drew back as he purposefully strode close. His proposition was blunt. "Come, let me in to you."

I had to fight back the urge to gasp, not only at his direct, base words, but at the fact I was successful in disguising myself. I glanced at Hirah. It was as if he was seeing through my festive robe. No real friend to Judah was he.

It was expected that I ask something in return for his sexual gratification. I willed myself to ask in a calm voice, lower and slower to be sure to cloak my identity.

"What will you give me that you may come in to me?"

"I'll send you a young goat from my flock."

"Only if you give me something as a pledge until you send it." I replied.

"What pledge should I give you?"

I could hardly control my pounding heart. I was hearing these words in the familiar voice of my father-in-law, the man at whose table I shared celebrations, the man I once thought would be my protector. His weathered face looked old and twisted. His eyes were full of lust, his voice gruff with sensual desire. Summoning the thought that our gods approved this, suppressing my sense of repulsion in every fiber of my body, I pressed on.

"Your seal and its cord, and the staff in your hand." I answered. The seal that hung around his neck was his personal stamp to confirm his identity on any binding agreement or message. The top of his staff was crafted for him alone.

He gave me these things. What followed I have barred completely from my memory. I only remember returning to the grove of trees and taking off that robe and veil that I would burn as soon as I could. Putting on my widow's clothes again, this garment that most would dread wearing, now felt like my cocoon of safety. I remember that I had to empty my stomach alongside the road on my walk back to my father's house. The bile of my vomit was sweeter than Judah's mouth. I bathed and was grateful when night fell when I could wrap myself in my own coverlet.

From this day forward, I would trust no one but God with my tomorrow.

Tamar's walk back to her father's house must have been full of self-questioning. Yes, she was trusting in the laws as she knew them. But she also knew her neighbors, Judah's family and friends. She had already experienced that they concluded what they wished about her character. Some thought her possessed and able to bring death to any who "knew" her. Her future? Unknown. And yet, she felt a stirring, a strong sense that she would bear a child. The sense infusing her soul was one of comfort regardless of the unknowns ahead.

———

Whether Judah was honoring his commitment of a kid goat for his pleasures or just wanted his personal possessions back, I do not know. He would keep his agreement with the "temple prostitute" he believed me to be. He sent his friend, Hirah, with the kid to make the transaction. Would that Hirah kept Judah from evil rather than being his accomplice. Word filtered back to me that Hirah was asking where the prostitute might be. The townspeople told him there was no such woman here. Hirah was no doubt puzzled, as he saw me himself. His only option was to simply bring that news to his friend. Judah had to decide whether to risk his reputation asking further about the location of this "prostitute," who seemed now not to exist.

Judah was quick to decide and I knew what that decision would be. Hirah, in a moment after too much wine, would tell his friends of Judah's dilemma. Judah would no doubt clap Hirah on the back stating, "I'll be laughed at for caring about keeping my word to a prostitute. The town says there is no such woman. I'll look like a fool. Let her keep what she has."

About three months later, my father-in-law was told I was pregnant due to whoredom.

Did he still blame me for the deaths of his sons? Did he excuse the evil his sons did? Did he remember what HE did on the way to the sheep shearing festival? His response was: "Bring her out and have her burned to death!"

I knew this moment might come. I had come to know the character of Judah and his sons. Only for a second did I think perhaps death by fire would be at least a known end to my sorrow-filled life. But another sense grew even greater through my months of early morning sickness and my sure sense of a caring presence hovering over me. The life growing in me was precious, not to be sacrificed to Baal, but to be born to be the person the true God intended. I no longer trusted the gods. I trusted one God, the God of Judah, even though Judah himself did not heed His directions.

It was time to take the ultimate risk. As I was about to be taken to the town center to be publicly burned at the stake, I grabbed my stricken father's arm. In the few weeks since we had the sure knowledge of my pregnancy, I saw him struggle with shame that would be his in our clan, and a tenderness twisted with disbelief as he looked at me. I had always sensed that I was his favorite daughter. My life tested him sorely. If I could have taken away his pain, surely I would have.

Before he could pull his arm back from my grasp, I pressed the seal with its chord and the staff into his shaking hands. "Take these to my father-in-law with these words: 'I am pregnant by the man who owns these.' See if you recognize whose seal and cord and staff these are."

My father's countenance changed to granite. Then an anger filled his eyes like nothing I had ever seen. He pressed through the gathering crowd to Judah. No longer stricken with grief and disbelief, he grasped what he knew to be Judah's seal. It had been stamped on the marriage document of his beautiful, curious, trusting daughter twice. He grasped Judah's staff, willing himself not to strike the man with it.

A crowd gathered. People from both clans hurried to the public place. Friends, relatives, curious onlookers, and those who had a thirst to see people at their most ugly—the moment they lit another human on fire.

Judah stood near the stake that was soon to be lit with me tied to it. He, it was presumed, had suffered the greatest indignation for my behavior. I stood slightly behind the crowd with an accuser holding each arm. I turned slightly so I could see Judah as my father approached him. Everyone stepped back to let my father through. Only one part of a staff protruded from his tunic. With his face inches from Judah's, he withdrew from under his cloak the rest of the staff, the chord, and its seal. He let the seal sway a bit near Judah's face. With a booming voice hoarse with emotion, he pronounced for the entire crowd to hear: "My daughter, Tamar, is with child, pregnant by the owner of these."

The shock of recognition swept Judah's face. Those nearest recognized the familiar staff head. Recognizing the ugly truth, through the hush, the words spread like a soft wave through the crowd.

"She is righteous, I am not. Since I wouldn't give her to my son Shelah." He said it loudly enough that many heard those words. I only cared that my father heard them.

The crowd parted as my father turned on his heel and strode back. Then, as though he sensed where I was, he turned my way, quickening his step. I ran into his open arms not caring who was staring, not caring whether Judah lived, died, brought me to his house, or disowned me. I had only one capable protector: God Himself.

According to custom, Judah sent for me to move into his home. He could have taken me to himself and slept with me. He did not.

In due time, I gave birth to twins. As the first one was about to be delivered, his hand came out first and the midwife tied a red string around it. The little hand withdrew, and a different son was born first. Perez had arrived first and Zerah afterward with the crimson thread on his arm.

My elation at having two sons was greater than the memory of the heaviness and discomfort of the last months of pregnancy. The pains of giving birth to twins was nothing compared to my joy looking deeply into their eyes as they nursed.

I was told that Judah changed after that moment. I was told he more closely lived as our God wished him to. That mattered little to me. I had two healthy sons to raise. I hungered to raise them as my God would wish. That would take the rest of my life. I wished for nothing more.

———

Sadly, Tamar never knew the tender love of a man who put her interests, pleasure, and protection above his own desires.

No more is told of her life raising her twins. Twice widowed, she twice mothered. Judah acknowledged his ownership as father of the twins, Perez and Zerah, and that she was more righteous than he. Rather than being a prostitute, she was acting according to God's accepted provisions for passing on the family inheritance and land.

History confirms this as she is mentioned in the Book of Ruth, and was in the lineage of King David. I Chronicles 2: 4 lists Judah's five sons, Er, Onan, Shelah, Perez, and Zeran. Matthew 1: 3-6 includes their lineage in the line of King David.

Tamar's story is curious, misunderstood, and one seldom discussed, nor a popular teaching topic. However, this widow's son, Perez, is in the lineage of David and more importantly, Jesus Christ. God had a very specific plan to provide for widows. Judah, Tamar, her husband and his brothers knew that plan. If your husband died and you had no children, his brothers or close relatives were responsible for taking you as their wife to produce heirs. When Tamar's husband died, Judah did not follow through. Tamar neither tricked Judah, nor violated God's plan for her. Judah stated, "She is more righteous than I."

What empowers a widow to take the kind of risk that Tamar did? Trust, not in herself, or those around her, but in God, Whom she had come to trust. Courage. Courage to take a risk that could have a terrible ending. Courage knowing that following God's plan was the best regardless of other's judgment. She is really no risk taker who is totally dependent on God.

STUDY GUIDE
GENESIS 38

Tamar is perhaps the most maligned and misunderstood widow in the Bible. One reason is that the accepted practices of land ownership and provision for widows of the time are foreign to us. Agrarian cultures were land-dependent for livelihood and survival. Land was inherited through generations, being passed from father to son. This was accepted practice among God's people and most other cultures around them. If a man died childless, it was his brother's obligation to provide an heir through his widow. If no brother did this, it reverted to her father-in-law. We may find this abhorrent, but that was reality in Tamar's day.

Rather than Tamar taking matters into her own hands, she trusted God's method of provision. Though God's people were not honoring his wishes, this Canaanite widow did.

David and Absalom both named their daughters after Tamar. Names were given based on the integrity they carried. Generations following Tamar recognized that she was a righteous woman, not what some have wrongly labeled her today.

Judah got a wife for Er, his firstborn, and her name was Tamar. But Er, Judah's firstborn, was wicked in the Lord's sight; so the Lord put him to death.

Then Judah said to Onan, "Sleep with your brother's wife and fulfill your duty to her as a brother-in-law to raise up offspring for your brother." But Onan knew that the child would not be his; so whenever he slept with his brother's wife, he spilled his semen on the ground to keep from providing offspring for his brother. What he did was wicked in the Lord's sight; so the Lord put him to death also.

Judah then said to his daughter-in-law Tamar, "Live as a widow in your father's household until my son Shelah grows up." For he thought, "He may die too, just like his brothers." So Tamar went to live in her father's household (Gen. 38: 6-11).

When Judah saw her, he thought she was a prostitute, for she had covered her face. Not realizing that she was his daughter-in-law, he went over to her by the roadside and said, "Come now, let me sleep with you."

"And what will you give me to sleep with you?" she asked.

"I'll send you a young goat from my flock," he said.

"Will you give me something as a pledge until you send it?" she asked.

He said, "What pledge should I give you?"

"Your seal and its cord, and the staff in your hand," she answered. So he gave them to her and slept with her, and she became pregnant by him. After she left, she took off her veil and put on her widow's clothes again (Gen. 38: 15-19).

About three months later Judah was told, "Your daughter-in-law Tamar is guilty of prostitution, and as a result she is now pregnant."

Judah said, "Bring her out and have her burned to death!"

As she was being brought out, she sent a message to her father-in-law. "I am pregnant by the man who owns these," she said. And she added, "See if you recognize whose seal and cord and staff these are."

Judah recognized them and said, "She is more righteous than I, since I wouldn't give her to my son Shelah." And he did not sleep with her again.

When the time came for her to give birth, there were twin boys in her womb. As she was giving birth, one of them put out his hand; so the midwife took a scarlet thread and tied it on his wrist and said, "This one came out first." But when he drew back his hand, his brother came out, and she said, "So this is how you have broken out!" And he was named Perez. Then his brother, who had the scarlet thread on his wrist, came out. And he was named Zerah (Gen. 38: 24-30).

STUDY QUESTIONS

1. Consider the realities of today. Is skewed labeling still prevalent? What actions should we take when this happens?
2. What labels were placed on Tamar?
3. What was Judah's final "label" for Tamar?
4. In what ways did Tamar display strength and courage?
5. Consider Tamar's plight as twice widowed. What benefits do singles have today?

THINKING IT OVER

Tamar's story illustrates people's tendency to judge others. And seldom are all the facts known or understood in proper perspective.

God has clear instruction on this.

Do not judge, so that you may not be judged. For with the judgment you make you will be judged, and the measure you give will be the measure you get. Why do you see the speck in your neighbor's eye, but do not notice the log in your own eye? Or how can you say to your neighbor, "Let me take the speck out of your eye," while the log is in your own eye? You hypocrite, first take the log out of your own eye, and then you will see clearly to take the speck out of your neighbor's eye (Mt. 7: 1-5 NRSV).

...on the day when, according to my gospel, God, through Jesus Christ, will judge the secret thoughts of all (Rom. 2: 16 NRSV).

There is one lawgiver and judge who is able to save and to destroy. So who, then, are you to judge your neighbor? (James 4: 12 NRSV)

PERSONAL APPLICATION

1. If you have been misunderstood, consider giving grace and mercy to those who neither knew nor understood your unique circumstances.

2. Recognize that no other human being can accurately empathize with another. God does, and needing to go to Him alone is a good thing.

3. Though others may neither understand nor grant you mercy and grace, remember God always does.

ELEVEN

RESILIENT
Bathsheba—Nonconsensual Intimacy, Murder, Yet Blessed

II Samuel 11:1-26, II Samuel 12: 24

SPRING TIME, WHEN KINGS GO OFF TO WAR

Bathsheba hurried to the main thoroughfare. More than spring was in the air. Excitement, the parade of warriors, horses, and carts filled with supplies. David's army filled the street. Led by Joab, they were formidable, striding behind him in order of their rank and prowess. They were leaving to subdue yet another neighbor. Having ravaged the Ammonites they would besiege their city of Rabbah.

In King David's passion to subdue all who were not God's people in his land, he pushed his armies to bold extremes. Beside his own cunning, strength, and sheer, almost mad determination, David could pick leaders, warriors who were like him, and loyal. The process of selecting the top thirty was about more than strength and speed. One had to be willing to kill. Killing was not the mark of a brutal, evil warrior, but rather a calling to protect

179

one's people for the honor of God. Warriors would compete for position, but protect one another in battle. There was only one rule greater than unity on the battlefield; absolute obedience and loyalty to King David. Uriah was such a man.

Bathsheba's husband was among King David's thirty select warriors. She pushed through the crowds to see those near the front. There, her Uriah! Any woman would see him as magnificent. For just one moment, she caught his eye. He was her husband, her tender lover, a man of such character that had he not been such a mighty warrior, he would still be respected for his trustworthiness and loyalty. Her eyes took in his broad shoulders, his stride of confidence. He exuded strength.

Those who knew his wife, Bathsheba, would say she was seen as desirable, beautiful, that Uriah was lucky to have her. No doubt the sons born to them would be magnificent.

Uriah's high position in David's army earned him special favors. He was rewarded with a home near the king's palace. For the sake of convenience and greater security, the king's mightiest men and their families lived in close community. Not that the privilege mattered to Bathsheba. She would have lived anywhere gladly with her Uriah.

Nearing the city gate, the crowd was so dense she could no longer move forward. Yet she watched until he was out of sight.

The ache in her heart willed her to return to their home. Climbing the steep ascent through the narrow streets, she entered the home Uriah brought her to after their marriage. Her mind replayed that celebration. Uriah, his family, and his groomsmen came to her father's home as was the custom, to claim her as his bride. Her father prepared a special room for the consummation of their marriage. While the guests ate, drank, and laughed Uriah tenderly carried her to that room. Spilling out into the courtyard the guests celebrated, rattled tambourines, and danced. None of that mattered to the new bride. What she remembered was being loved by Uriah.

She pushed back the curtain and threw herself on their bed. Burying her head in their bed covering, she breathed the scent of his body and sobbed. How long would he be gone this time? His departure would have been easier had they had a child by now. But even though Uriah had been relieved of going out to war for one year after their marriage, as was their custom, there was no baby yet.

Hadn't some prophet told her father she would bear a son who would be king someday? Enough—she rose to face the days ahead alone.

Her older sister needed her. Bathsheba hurried back down the steep path to the home of Elizabeth, who had three small children and was heavy again with child. There were loaves to bake, clothes to wash, and water to carry. Thankfully, Bathsheba tousled the children's hair and welcomed the activity to fill her days until Uriah returned.

Elizabeth teased her sister giving her a knowing look. "You are not with child yet?"

"We'll catch up," Bathsheba answered with more assurance in her voice than in her heart.

At dusk, Bathsheba returned to her home. She was grateful now for her location. This place of status near the palace meant her neighbors shared life's lonely challenges of being married to a warrior. Wives of the others in King David's thirty were her neighbors. They greeted her. It was a place of safety and community; devoid of their men, the women chatted with each other. If they shared the same fears, they were unspoken. After all, David's thirty seemed invincible.

While King David could look down from his palace on the homes tucked into the hill beneath him, they could see nothing of his abode due to the steep incline and overhanging rooftops. But they sensed the safety of being near the palace.

Days passed. Evenings were quiet. The time of monthly uncleanness came. Bathsheba hid her disappointment. She so desperately wanted, upon Uriah's return from battle, to be able to tell him she was with child. Not this time. At dusk, her monthly uncleanness ended, and as was the custom she went to her courtyard to bathe. Water could be poured on the ground there. Animals were collected for security. It was a place of familiar comfort. Cool water soothed her from the heat of the day, and the emptiness in her soul. Wiping herself sparingly since water was scarce, she went back to the silent stillness for yet another night alone.

While preparing a simple meal for herself, she heard a brisk, hard rap on her door. Wrapping her shawl tightly, she opened it a bit. Would a military messenger bring dreaded news? She puzzled at the sight of two men from David's palace. They simply stated her presence was requested. She examined their faces. There was neither compassion—as if they knew bad news of Uriah but could not state it—nor respect due to Uriah's position. Their faces were hard and inscrutable.

This request made no sense. Uriah was one of David's trusted mighty men at the front of his battles. David could be trusted.

As they approached the palace, Bathsheba felt a shiver of uncertainty. They were not approaching one of the main entrances, but an obscure back door. Still she followed. Two messengers? No words? Through narrow hallways, she was finally led into a room with beauty beyond her imagination. Tapestries covered the walls. An ornate wooden carved couch with matching chairs, a table with golden wine goblets. Then, the shock of recognition. Surely not. Behind hanging tapestries she saw a bed.

The urge to flee coursed through her. Glancing over her shoulder she knew she could not. The two men's faces were like chiseled stone.

The door on the opposite side of the room opened. David walked in sparsely clothed. His eyes revealed his intent. Horrified, I could neither run nor refuse his advances. He was the king. His messengers bowed to him and backed out of the room.

As his eyes raked my body it was as if he were a different man. There was no jubilant smile as when he addressed us as his people. There was no look of compassion as when he learned of his people's hardships. I had never seen such a narrow, hard look of lust. While others thought of him as appealing in appearance, he was nothing compared to my Uriah. Even had he been, to think of lying with anyone other than my beloved was revolting. I would close my eyes, close my mind, and will my body not to feel. But before willing my mind to numbness, I said to myself, "I am Bathsheba, true wife of Uriah. I am not an adulterer."

I don't remember any of his words as he drew me into his bed. He grasped my hands harshly and raised them over my head. I felt pinned as an object, not a person, beneath him. I would feel no more. The night seemed like an endless nightmare.

Just hours before dawn, there was a knock at the rear door. David handed Bathsheba her robe and glanced away from her look of revulsion and disbelief. He opened the door, and the same two men escorted her back to her home.

Anguish, fear, anger, disgust. I could hardly stand. I rushed to my water jug, threw all that was left over my body, scrubbed, yet I felt filthy. Uriah, oh, my Uriah! Over and over I called his name, wept, grabbed the bed coverings, and lay on the floor. I dared not lay again in the bed I shared with my beloved Uriah. I feared my ravaged body would destroy all our marriage had been and could never be again.

Disbelief. Replaying those hours. Could I have refused? Screamed for help? For days, I sent word to Elizabeth that I was needed by an ill neighbor. Unable to eat or sleep, my mind raced in circles. Who would defy or challenge the king and his actions? Besides the two escorts, who else knew? Whoredom. Adultery. Punishable by death. Worse than that thought was that my life as it had been with Uriah was over. Impossible. That complete trust and total abandon lying together would never be again. I knelt by our bed. I dared not lie in it, defiled as I had been by the king.

Each night I lay down on the floor mat. I reached up to touch the bed we had shared. Would death be more welcome than this despair? Eventually I slept fitfully, dreaming of Uriah valiantly fighting somewhere to protect me, to come home to me, for life to go on.

I entered Elizabeth's home. More than the usual disarray greeted me. Thankfully, I was needed here. When Elizabeth wrapped me in a hug, my shoulders shrugged, shuddering slightly. Pulling back, Elizabeth looked deeply into my face. This was not the sister she last saw. Disheveled, unwilling for our usual eye contact to linger, this was not her free spirited sister and friend. I tore into kneading the bread with few words and not the usual banter with my nieces and nephews.

Every morning I was ill. Surely it was brought on by being distraught. Disgust was replaced by fear. I remembered the messengers who knew. And who else? I could not eat. When I tried, my body rejected even the plainest morsel of bread.

The walk to Elizabeth's was especially hot this day. I bent over the laundry in her courtyard scrubbing the children's clothing. Feeling a bit light headed was the last thing I remembered.

Bathsheba, Bathsheba! Elizabeth was cradling my head in her arms. She touched cool water to my lips. Her precious children were staring at me. Even great with child, she was stronger than me and helped me struggle to my feet. I dropped to a mat in the shade of her home. Her eyes looked through me and told me the reality I could not deny. I was pregnant.

The next day Elizabeth came to my door uninvited, yet so welcome. No sooner had she entered than I threw myself into her arms wailing. For moments there were no words. And then as if a dam broke in my spirit, I poured out to her the horrible truth. I searched her eyes praying to see that look of love and easy acceptance we shared since childhood.

She gently took my face in her hands and whispered, "Bathsheba, my little precious beautiful lamb. You are no adulterer. The guilt is on the king. God be merciful to this babe. And rescue you from harm."

We talked as only sisters could of all the possibilities. What was wise? What were the risks? All would soon know. What must be done?

Perhaps naïvely, I decided the king should know quickly. While Elizabeth was not as convinced as I, she stepped out and asked my neighbor if any of the king's messengers were nearby. I wrote three words on a bit of parchment, folded it, and waited. Elizabeth clasped me tightly and insisted I come to her home the next day. As she left, one of the king's messengers approached. I recognized him from that fateful night.

Was there a touch of compassion in his gaze this time? I could tell he was willing himself to show no emotion.

"Kindly take this message to the king." He took to the steep path up to the palace in almost a run.

The next weeks were puzzling. I was told by a messenger that Uriah would come home from the battlefield. I no longer tried to justify anything the king did with good intent. Even warriors summoned home during wartime were not to know their wives. They were set apart and focused only on fighting. Unity and bravery was devoting yourself fully to the battle, denying yourself any comfort; that was the warrior code. I knew Uriah, man of honor that he was, would not come to my bed. Foolish David! His plotting would be for naught. Of that I was certain.

I was right. I had friends in the king's court and word filtered back. Uriah brought his report and was given a gift. But he did not come to me, or even approach our home. He slept at the entrance to the king's house with the servants. He did send David's gift to me. It was a basket of delicacies: dates, figs, and fine cheese. I burned it.

Word was that Uriah was asked to stay with King David another day. But those who knew what they did that day were quiet. My suspicions of the king grew. My distrust grew to loathing.

I knew he was sent back to battle with a message from David for Joab, the head of his army.

I decided to spend the next days at Elizabeth's home. I could no longer even bear to sleep on the floor beside the bed that Uriah and I shared. The bustle of her household, though exhausting, was better than the silence of mine. I had only been there a few days adjusting to their life there when I heard again a determined rap on their door. I knew before the door opened that the king's messengers were here.

"Uriah, your husband, has been killed in battle." Their words pierced like a knife. Elizabeth's arms around my waist kept me from falling.

"He fought valiantly. The king sends his deepest regrets." I tried to mouth an acknowledgment but could make no sound. Elizabeth managed a soft "thank you" and closed the door.

My Uriah killed. Killed in battle. I sank to the floor unable to calm the storm in my mind. Despair waged with hot anger. Disbelief succumbed to a sure conviction that David was as responsible for Uriah's murder as if he had shot the arrows himself. Elizabeth took the children into the courtyard. I huddled on the floor, back against the wall, hugging my knees, unsure I could rise again.

The next day I returned to my home, covering myself with the robes of a widow. What was usually a short walk seemed forever. With every step my heart rebelled. My destination seemed no longer my home, but a place once inhabited by two people I no longer knew. My neighbors came mourning and wailing. They brought food and attempted words of comfort. When my days of mourning were over, David sent for me.

Moving into King David's palace was a nightmare in my soul that I had to hide. Most women came gladly. Living in wealth, having servants and status, most were eager to settle into a life of safety, no trips to wells for water, no kneading bread, collecting sticks for fires. Few had come from lives as pleasant as living as the wife of King David.

Not me. I did not come gladly. Pregnant with David's child, grieving the death of my beloved Uriah, I was sent for after the allotted time of mourning was over. Still wearing my black coverings, I wanted to wear them forever, sleep every night on the bed Uriah and I shared, knowing he could no longer be hurt by the tragedy in my life. I would push the discomforts of pregnancy from my mind, forget David's look of lust as he lay with me. I wanted to live in the memory of Uriah forever.

I remember vividly being taken back to the king's palace, now to become his wife. Servants bowed and his messengers nodded, acknowledging my position.

Puzzling. I was David's seventh wife. But they brought me to a location of greater status than that. Abigail's quarters were nearby. Beautiful robes were laid out with servant girls at my disposal. I did not care. Thankfully, at evening time, I could huddle under my coverlet and disappear into the world of sleep.

I felt myself curling up, sliding my back into Uriah's strong chest and shoulders, feeling his gentle strength as he wrapped his arms around me. I breathed deeply to take in his familiar scent. But his scent was missing. Instead an image appeared of my Uriah sprawled bloodied and dying, arrows piercing every part of his body that I had caressed, blood oozing, covering the ground around him. I screamed.

Beautiful Abigail was hovering over me. "Bathsheba, my child. You must have had a nightmare." Tears streamed down my cheeks, the taste of bile rose in my mouth. "Quick!" she admonished the servant girl. "Bring a basin." Emptied of its bitter contents, my stomach still ached, but not as much as my soul.

She came again the next day. Her eyes spoke compassion. She asked questions and listened. She invited me to join her as she went about supervising some of the many projects under her authority. I accepted, grateful to have something to do with the empty hours, grateful to be in the company of Abigail. We became friends.

Some might think us an unlikely pair as friendships go. Word of how she met David traveled via chatter at the wells and through our wives' courtyard. Had her first husband, Nabal, been as terrible as the gossip made him out to be? Word also was that her skill as an overseer was extensive. She understood flocks, and oversaw the process from healthy animals to prepared meat. She oversaw plantings, produce from trees, and land plots. More importantly, all the servants respected her: women and men. She was an industrious overseer. She was trusted.

I followed her as she went through the king's gardens. She explained plants and what they were used for. My ears heard, my mind did not grasp. The cloak of grief, the shock of my husband's brutal death, still held my mind in their grip. Little did I know the joy of giving birth would not end my dance with death.

Weeks became months. I could not eat. The nightmares continued, but were less vivid. My once attractive prominent cheekbones protruded from hollow cheeks. Abigail took notice.

"Bathsheba, my friend, I have delegated my duties this morning. Let's just spend time in the garden instead." We settled into one of her favorite spots. She looked at me intently. "Talk to me about Uriah," she said softly. Tears flowed immediately. I'd not spoken his name to another since coming to the king's palace. A torrent of words flowed. My first sight of him, our families' intentional planning, pride of his skill as one of David's mighty men. My hunger for all marriage would bring. Our marriage, our first love making. His desire, my desire. Our first year with him home. Our plans, my fears when he went off to war. My thrill when he returned. The times I was by his side when David invited his mighty men to his palace. My confidence in my king. And then.

I could not stop. I poured out my horror at being taken in lust only, by the king, one Uriah trusted, one to whom Uriah was loyal. The disbelief of pregnancy. Uriah's return to sleep outside the king's home with the servants rather than dishonor the vow of a soldier at war. How a troubling thought entered my mind that David was scheming. Surely not. God's anointed? Then

Uriah left again for battle. The knock at my door. Messengers from the king. Something in my heart shuddered even as I looked at their faces. Not Uriah, not my Uriah.

I could no more halt the torrent of words than I could reverse the life and growth of the babe within me.

Abigail listened as I poured out what they told me of my husband's death, his murder at the hands of enemies. They brought his body back. Common warriors were buried at the battle sight. David's most valuable leaders were brought back to a designated burial ground outside the palace wall. I was not allowed to touch his precious cold cheek. In fact, I was not even allowed to see him.

Could these cruel rumors be true? Whispers from those who knew Joab well. Friends of Uriah's who had been on the front line. Men told to draw back without Uriah's knowledge. Men told to violate their oath of loyalty to each other in battle. Only a direct order from the king would result in Uriah's trusted fellow soldiers abandoning him to King David's enemies. My mind did not want to accept those thoughts. But my heart confirmed they were true.

Abigail kept listening. She did not shush me, object, or defend. She just listened. Finally, spent and hardly able to breathe, I collapsed into her tender arms. She simply held me until I could sob no more.

I saw no look of accusation in her eyes like I saw in other wives of David. I saw no scorn like I saw in the eyes of David's messengers. I saw understanding. She was still my friend.

Graciously, she did not speak to me about Nabal, her marriage, even David at that time. She simply listened to my story.

I sensed inner healing after that time with Abigail. We began to share mealtimes. My appetite returned. My baby grew. We could talk about what was ahead. How fortunate I am to have such a wise friend. While I would have liked many sister-like friendships in the palace, the other wives looked at Abigail and me with jealousy. We were both gifted by God with beauty and favoritism from the king. But with that came pain they could not imagine, which drew us even closer. She became my palace sister.

Weeks passed, and I thought of what I'd heard of Nabal, Abigail's first husband. I was curious if what I'd heard was true. At her side as she walked through the drying flax on the rooftop of one of the many buildings, I noted her comments to people working. They listened with respect. I wanted to be like Abigail. "May we go to the garden for a bit?" I asked. She nodded.

We settled into our favorite corner. I felt awkward with my protruding body trying to get comfortable on our mat. "Tell me about Nabal," I said.

She looked at me as if she saw my thoughts and began. The rumors were accurate. "He was an angry, brash man, a hard man to please, but cunning enough to see that it was to his advantage to give me free reign. I could see that his servants would sabotage his directions unless I became the one to whom they would answer. They feared him with good reason."

She told me of how she listened to the news of her country. She had not known of the early days of King Saul when he'd been a humble man. She knew of a king who had some victories in battle, but increasingly was given to bouts of depressing anger. She also had heard that it was the will of the people for David to be king. His reputation shown brighter, his character was more in keeping with what God expected. It was believed that the prophet Samuel had secretly anointed him earlier. King Saul became jealous and vengeful, and fell from God's favor. Abigail told me she took note, but had no time to ponder these events. Nabal's continuing outbursts and the scope of her increasing responsibilities consumed her.

All knew shepherds roamed with their sheep into possibly unwelcome places. They went where the pastures provided plenty. Those living in the area would steal from them when they could, a lamb here, a wandering sheep there. Nabal's shepherds had moved into the hill country where David and his men were hiding. Rather than stealing from Nabal, David's men defended and protected them.

In return, when the shepherds brought the sheep back for shearing, David requested a "gift," an appropriate response to his protection. Not only did Nabal refuse, he insulted God's anointed.

———

"The story of Nabal's insults to David prompted me to do what would be unthinkable to many wives: act without my husband's permission, even knowledge. I had become accustomed to being the initiator, negotiator, and implementer over the household and the overseer of much of our flocks.

"In Nabal's sober moments he would tell me that any man would be glad to be honored as he was, as my husband. Yes, his eyes saw my appearance, but also revealed respect. Had I loved him at one time? I can't remember. I only knew bloodshed was ahead. David's reputation was of utmost importance."

A look of intensity filled Abigail's eyes. "I would sooner do my God's bidding at the risk of punishment, even death at Nabal's hands, than not honor the truth I knew. David, as a brash young king, should not have revenge blood on his hands."

She paused long and took a deep breath. "Even now David's intensity, his impulsive desires can...." My friend did not need to finish the sentence. The babe I carried was evidence that her words were true.

I awoke to the feel of warm water in my bed. I turned to rise, but a sharp pain beyond anything I'd ever experienced stabbed my back and encircled my abdomen. I could not stifle my cry.

A midwife entered quickly. "It's time," she said softly. "Follow my every word and all will be well." She knew the bag of waters that surrounded my babe in my womb breaking meant a short but very hard labor. I could only look and nod with fear. Thankfully, Abigail entered and took my hand. Simply her presence calmed my soul even though my body was overtaken by waves of the spasms of childbirth.

I was shocked at the intensity of labor. Mercifully, mine was short due to the bag of waters breaking first. When the midwife laid my tiny boy on my breast, I could not take my eyes off him. Dark intense eyes like mine, a tuft of reddish hair. No baby could be more beautiful.

Instinctively he searched to nurse and as he did so I placed my finger in his hand. His tiny fingers grasped mine with all his strength.

All my tumultuous emotions of the past melted. I would love my son forever. He would have the best of life I could provide. David could not help but love him too.

Within a few days, David sent for us. I wore the royal robe he provided. My son was wrapped in the softest of all wool blankets. I approached his throne and knelt, remembering how Abigail taught me to address him as king.

"My lord, here is your son."

He lifted him tenderly and then tucked him in his arm looking at him an overlong time. I wondered his thoughts, but knew I would need to be content to never know.

I was thankful for the servants, the midwife, and their attention. But more precious was the friendship of Abigail. Now the mother of two, she offered me her wisdom. No question was avoided.

I hoped now for days of quiet and peace with my son. On the fourth day after his birth, I walked slowly with Abigail as she supervised the selection of wool to be spun for royal robes. Thankfully, our walk was short and I was glad to be carrying my babe in his pouch rather than lumbering with him heavy within me. Fatigued for sure, but seeing this place with new eyes, I thought of all the possibilities of raising my son here. I was beginning to make peace with this new life.

We were returning through an outer court when Abigail took my arm and stopped me.

"That's the prophet Nathan," she said. He paused and looked at us knowingly and seemed to look over long at my babe. Gazing back at me, I could not fathom his thoughts. He turned and walked resolutely toward the court where David sat. We knew the presence of a prophet was important as Adonai never sent messages not of import. But we were not welcome to enter unless invited. I was glad to go back to my chamber.

Nathan's visit seemed to have brought an uproar of rumors. Hardly had he left before people were hurrying from King David's court. Wives and concubines were hurrying out into the women's courtyard where news was spread most quickly. I would lie on my bed at least for a few moments. News mattered little to me. The unknowns of my life were behind me, both the anticipated future with Uriah, his death, and David's impregnating me. Past. Today I have a healthy son. I will be his protector, his teacher, and nurture him to be a great man.

It seemed too quiet in our empty chambers. Why were the women not returning with their chatter? The news must be either important or intriguing. I picked up my babe to join the others and listen.

As I entered the courtyard, a hush fell. Never were David's wives and concubines this quiet. And why when I entered? I approached Abigail. She gently touched my shoulder and whispered, "Let's go back inside." She led me to her chamber, which was larger than mine. We sat on her bed. She leaned close and spoke so quietly I strained to hear her.

"David should be sending for you to tell you Nathan's words. But I know him. He will not. Yet you must know. Nathan spoke to David in a parable of sorts. He spoke of a poor man who had only one ewe lamb he raised and cherished. In fact the lamb joined his family at meal times and was loved like a daughter. He spoke of a rich man who had many flocks and herds. A traveler came to the rich man's home. Hospitality dictated the rich man kill a sheep for the traveler's meal. The rich man did so. But he did not take one from his own herds. He took the precious ewe of the poor man and slaughtered it. He dined with his visitor savoring the best lamb he had ever eaten. He had no pity for the poor man whose sheep he had stolen and killed."

She paused. I looked at her only with questioning. Of what relevance was this to cause such a commotion in the women's chambers? And why would Abigail think David should be telling me this?

She continued. "Nathan asked the king, 'What should be done in a case like this?' David was livid. He shouted that the payback should be four times what was taken. Custom dictates twice what is taken. But David's anger was intense because the rich man had no pity. Greater than the theft was the disregard of the personhood and sense of great loss he inflicted on the poor man and his family."

I still looked on with questioning.

She looked away from me with troubling fear. It was as if she would not continue. She turned back and grabbed me by the shoulders. Words tumbled rapidly and she could no longer whisper. With all her effort she kept her voice as low as her emotions would allow.

"You are that man!" Nathan thundered this at our king! All feared David would order Nathan killed on the spot. But Nathan continued with a bold voice unlike any ever heard before the king. He recounted all God has given our king, the many times and ways Adonai has saved, spared, and protected him. He shouted, "God would have granted any of your requests!" Then Nathan became silent. He looked at David with such intensity that some wondered if David would faint from the gaze piercing his soul.

David's chamber was silent. No one moved or even breathed deeply.

Eventually Nathan continued.

"Why have you despised the word of the Lord, to do what is evil in his sight?"(II Sam. 12: 9 NRSV)

He gave no opportunity for David to answer.

Abigail wrapped me in her arms and in a hoarse whisper continued in my ear.

"Oh, dear Bathsheba, as our Lord lives these are Nathan's very words. 'You struck down Uriah the Hittite with the sword and took his wife to be your own. You killed him with the sword of the Ammonites. Now, therefore, the sword will never depart from your house, because you despised me and took the wife of Uriah the Hittite to be your own" (II Sam. 12: 9-10).

My soul recoiled in disbelief and shock that David's sins were now public. David killed my beloved. David killed. I had known that in my own soul. Now all of our kinsmen, our people, would know. Disbelief gave way again to anger, which was quickly displaced by hatred. I held my precious babe more closely. Abigail held me even more tightly.

I hardly heard the words that continued to spill from my friend. She was saying unthinkable things that would happen to our king. Their reality was nothing compared to mine. With white-hot anger, I would gather only what my babe and I needed and leave this city, this place. I would rather be at God's mercy traveling to an obscure place in the wilderness than live anywhere near this evil man.

Then Abigail's grip lessened. She took my face in her hands and whispered quietly now. "Are you listening? How I wish to not speak these next words. But these are truths about you for you. Adonai would want you to know. Nathan pronounced to David and in the hearing of all that the child you have borne will die because the king, David himself, has utterly scorned the Lord.ʺ

For a moment, I could not move. I knew Abigail would only speak truth to me. I rose with strength beyond my own, hurried to my own chamber. I dropped my royal robe and grabbed the widow garment I had worn coming in. Few knew I kept it. Wrapping my face tightly I took a few things my babe would need. Thankfully, our chambers were still empty. I left quickly avoiding the areas where guards might be. Even the usual guard posts were empty. The import of Nathan's message must be shaking to everyone.

I remembered the back narrow passageways I was led through nine months before. Swift and quiet, I was able to slip through that same obscure gate into the familiarity of the neighborhood outside the palace. I hurried in a circuitous way to the home Uriah and I had shared. Not daring to be seen at our front entryway, I slipped in the back of our courtyard.

Fearing eyes from above on that fateful hill, I slipped into our home. Had Elizabeth been here to freshen my home? It should have been dustier. There was water in our drinking jug. I drank deeply. I also was filled with a profound sense that Adonai was more than watching me. He was looking out for me.

Pushing my widow's robe under our bed, for the first time since that fateful night with David, I lay down on my bed, the one I shared with my lover, the only one who cherished me, the only one I would ever love, my Uriah. I gave my breast to my babe. The peace of vindication soothed me and brought me peace as I never had since that night. I thanked God for Nathan's bravery. Before dozing off, I made a plan. At evening time, before the city gates closed, I would slip out of this fateful city. I would take my chances at the mercy of Adonai, not those who lived here.

My babe's cry awakened me. Thankfully it was still daylight. I offered him my breast. He thrashed and refused to nurse. He was always calmed by my walking. I would gather what I needed and leave.

I wrapped myself in the drab flax garment I used to wear to the well. Concealing my widow's garments—they might provide me a needed disguise—I tucked my son next to my body. Thankfully his cries had subsided to moaning. I did not want to draw attention to myself.

Pausing to look around at the only space that mattered any more, memories flooded back. Uriah and I, fresh in love, dreaming, cherishing each other in every way we could, our tender nights before his leave-taking for battles. His safe return with tales I knew were only part of what he experienced on the battlefield.

I remembered celebrating quietly, just the two of us, after ceremonies in the palace where he was honored for his valor. I was so proud of my magnificent husband.

It was as if thunder interrupted my reverie. *My babe would die!* Abigail had spoken those words. She would not lie. Yes, I must escape this evil place. Deceit, needless murder. I could not stand to live here. But my babe! Could I protect him from God's judgment? When would he die? How? Could I intervene in God's will? Change His mind?

How long would we both live if I traveled to the wilderness to escape the chaos of this place?

I realized I needed to go to my sister.

Daylight was fast fading, for which I was grateful. Keeping my drab veil over most of my face, hiding my babe and small bag of belongings under my wrap, I retraced the steps so lightly taken in days gone by. Thankfully Elizabeth was alone in her courtyard when I slipped in. I motioned for her to be quiet. She nodded, disappeared inside for a moment, and returned. We sat in the darkening evening and spoke quietly.

Yes, she had heard the news of Nathan's visit to the king. Everyone had. No, she did not know what I should do. Leave the safety of the city for the wilderness? She looked at me as if I were mad. Yet, she understood, perhaps as no one but possibly Abigail could, that this was not a safe place for me.

My babe fussed. We were all exhausted. We both knew I could not enter her home. Her children and her husband would know and be questioned. She urged me to stay in the safety of their courtyard for the night. She brought a mat and coverlet, I huddled with my babe, nursing, looking up at the stars. What would tomorrow bring?

Was it my imagination that my babe shivered with a chill? We both slept.

Elizabeth awakened me. After her husband left for their field, she had taken her children to a friend's home. She guided me into her home, and I was thankful for warm bread and cheese. My babe refused to be nursed. He shivered. Elizabeth looked closely at him. She had never seen a babe whose lips were so blue. Our eyes met filled with deep concern.

Elizabeth was willing to supply me with food and water to start my journey. But she questioned why. Only from my trusted sister would I consider those words.

If my babe would not nurse and took ill, the best care would be in the palace. Only the best midwives and servants aided David's wives, concubines, and children. Was it my milk, my burden of stress causing this? Neither of us would speak of the possibility that God's pronouncement of death could be imminent.

I stayed in the quiet of her home pondering, puzzling, and pleading with God for wisdom. She went to fetch water. We needed to act before her family returned.

I watched my babe closely. It seemed his breathing was shallow and labored. I realized then with clarity what I needed to do. My babe was more important than my own life. I needed to return to the palace and face whatever the next days would bring. He might be granted healing there.

Elizabeth could see the resolve in my countenance the moment she stepped in the room. At dusk she would walk with me to the back entrance of the palace. I would show my face to the guard and that of my babe. Elizabeth would be witness that I had returned safely and willingly to King David.

Approaching the gate, the guard stepped forward to prevent this woman in a drab flax garment from entering. Elizabeth took my arm and I felt her strength. I stepped close and lowered my wrap to reveal my face. The guard quickly changed his look of surprise to an emotionless stare. I hugged Elizabeth, she kissed my babe, and I slipped quietly inside.

Relieved to have been stopped by no one on my way to my chamber, I entered with a determination to focus only on my babe until God fulfilled His word.

I decided to stay in my quarters. Servant girls brought delicacies. I sent the trays back untouched and asked for bread and goat's milk only. Abigail learned of my return and visited me, expressing relief.

"The king neither eats nor rises from the ground since Nathan's visit." This news did not matter to me. David seemed like no king to me. I offered my son to Abigail with pleading eyes. She, like Elizabeth, had never seen such blue lips. She held him close to her cheek listening to his shallow breaths. Then she spoke.

"He does not breathe the sweet smell of a healthy babe's breath."

My instinct would have me resist those words. But a resolve rolled quietly into my soul. My babe's life would be short. This I knew from Adonai.

I had seven precious days with my son. Abigail proved to be a friend beyond imagination. She rarely left my side. I slept little and could not take my eyes off my son. I heard his last breath. Felt his tiny body shudder slightly and become motionless. His face turned ashen grey. I nodded to my friend. She left the room to inform David's messengers.

I knew my son would soon be taken from me. I would forever treasure the moment I first laid eyes on him. I took his motionless tiny fingers and wrapped them around mine as he had done seven days before.

Two messengers entered. I laid my son in the arms of one. A dead babe to them, my firstborn would live forever in my heart.

I heard that King David had gone into the house of the Lord to worship again. I heard he had returned to his routines and duties. Women whispered as I passed through the courtyard.

Thankfully, I escaped the palace at Abigail's side to see the new vineyard she authorized and a flock she thought ready for shearing.

I had no idea what life would be like now. Rather than imagine or remember my shattered dreams, I spent hours with Abigail. No wonder she was respected. We went together where fruit was being dried for the king's table. She spoke to the foremen and servants with respect. Her directions were clear. She praised good work.

One morning we left early to inspect new lambs in a field outside the palace. Guards accompanied us for our safety. Being outside the palace was invigorating. In fact a longing to live elsewhere, anywhere tugged at my soul. Abigail's voice brought me to the present. She began describing what she would be looking for in the lambs. She instructed the foremen to separate those she thought should be fattened for the king's table. Others would become food for the workers and servants in the palace. It seemed there was no end to Abigail's industrious efforts. King David trusted her implicitly and she had freedoms few wives enjoyed.

Many of them would not have "enjoyed" the work as she did. They seemed content with inactivity and gossip. I found myself enjoying learning, thriving on the physical demands of her extensive projects. She encouraged me to communicate with the foremen as I gained insights. She laughed and told me one blessing of being Nabal's wife was the necessity of learning, the necessity of leading, instructing, being efficient. I admired her more with each passing day.

We came to hardly notice the looks of jealousy when we entered the wives' courtyard. Approaching my quarters, a messenger greeted me and stated simply, "The king has requested your presence tomorrow."

My disappointment at not spending the day with Abigail was small compared to my dread of what being in the "presence" of the king would be like. Being taken as Uriah's wife and impregnated was a terror I could not forget. Presenting him with our son only seven days after his birth to bury him was an inexplicable sadness. Tomorrow would be a day of bathing, servants combing and smoothing my hair, preparing me to please the desires of the king. Abigail wisely advised me. "He is but a man, Bathsheba. He has been humbled. Just as he has his moments of greatness, he is sometimes weak and does not even see the fault lines within his own family. He has created them himself by not attending to his own matters. Don't see him as a great warrior and king, though at times he is. See him as a man who might earn your loyalty, even though he may never earn your love."

I reviewed her words in my mind as I followed the king's messenger the next evening to dine with the king.

That evening was unlike anything I imagined or feared. A delicious dinner was spread for just the two of us. His greeting was emotional. He spoke of the beauty of our son, his great remorse for his sin against God and against me. He pledged to protect and provide for me. A man of many words, one word he never uttered was "Uriah."

King David asked my forgiveness! While I felt no affection for him, or obligation to forgive, I sensed I had the courage to do the right thing because of Adonai. I nodded and whispered my forgiveness.

This time, he took me tenderly. There was a bit of consolation in that.

I spent the entire night in his bed. When I awakened, he was gone. A servant maid entered with grapes and a delicious loaf. "You are invited to stay as long as you wish," she said, kneeling before me. I walked onto the veranda looking out on the bustling courtyard below. I sensed I did not belong here and went back into his chamber. I decided to enjoy this meal and ponder my future with this man. It was the first time I had allowed my mind to go there.

Abigail and I resumed our activities, but only for a short time. She was pregnant again and difficulties required complete rest. She urged me to continue oversight of the projects so important to her. I could not refuse my friend. I did so with growing confidence. Little did I realize this would enhance my position later as David's favorite wife. I learned more about the requirements of the palace: food for all at court, clothing for hundreds, fine wool for David's family and concubines, rough flax for others and servants. I brought back news and reports to Abigail valuing her insights.

I was not surprised when morning sickness signaled my pregnancy.

How different was the birth of Solomon. David and I both welcomed him as we had our first son. But in the sight of others, Solomon's standing was different. He would be watched as a potential heir to David's throne. I wished now for years of peace to raise and train Solomon and our children yet to come. Solomon would have teachers in writing and mathematics, instructors in weapons of war, and my overarching supervision to ensure he had every opportunity and privilege possible.

Peace in David's palace, in Jerusalem, and our country was fragile and temporary. He had forged an alliance of sorts between our northern brothers, the Israelites, and our people. Victories at war were his strength, his charisma an advantage at times. But he neglected his adult children. They were spoiled, arrogant, and self-seeking. Abigail and I both observed this. He did not welcome our words about any of his children but our own. And then he only wanted to hear of their strengths, success, and intelligence.

Unchecked, his children indulged any desire they had. Amnon and Absalom especially went to great lengths to gain the loyalty of the people, even to usurp their father's throne. Absalom set up his own court in Hebron, the very location where David took Abigail as his new bride. My friend could hardly tolerate the thought of David permitting such defiance. The conflict was so great we fled Jerusalem for our safety for a time.

David's defiance of Adonai's instructions was evident in the wives and concubines he took for himself. He decided to number people, his possible fighting men. God had specifically forbidden this. Abigail and I spoke of these matters knowing all of our nation might suffer for David's sins.

That time came quickly after the report came back on the number of our people.

Thankfully, David returned to his senses, but only after famine and plague raged through our country. I often wondered how God could bless him so. All knew the law of not taking foreign wives. And he had so many. I knew he permitted lust in his children. After all, his example spoke for itself.

Yet there were times when his faith was so utter and complete, his remorse and admittance of his sins so sincere, that I could see why God would relent in His promised punishments at David's pleading.

Such was the case after Absalom's death. God revealed Himself again to David on Mount Moriah. King David purchased a threshing floor there, sacrificed to our God, and pledged to build His permanent altar there.

No human could tell David "no," but God did. His words were, "You have shed much blood and have fought many wars. You are not to build a house for my Name, because you have shed much blood on the earth in my sight" (I Chronicles 22: 80).

I knew David would carry this disappointment to his grave. God did permit him to assemble all that would be needed for His temple. The rest of his life he pursued that mission only. He avoided the great responsibility of identifying his successor.

I had become respected among everyone in the palace complex, including his advisors and our prophet. David's decline became evident. His avoidance of the ascendency of kingship was unsettling to our people. Just when Adonijah, one of his sons, was nearing success at securing the throne, the prophet Nathan approached me.

He urged my immediate action with convincing words. "If you do not act, Adonijah will become king and kill you and Solomon." We both knew David well. Our approach to him was planned and executed carefully.

I approached David in his room. Abishag, the beautiful young woman chosen to lie with him to keep him warm, respectfully withdrew. How different this was from approaching him on his throne, summoned at times to sit beside him in my own elegant seat, receiving the bows of those who revered him. I approached this old man in his room with confidence. The lives of my four sons and the futures of my daughters were precarious. He knew of my position of respect in the kingdom. At his old age, I doubted he even remembered the beginnings of our life together. That no longer mattered to me. Time and circumstance—children, kingdoms, life itself, softens, even erases memories.

I reminded my king of his promise that Solomon would inherit the throne. I described to him the imminent danger of Adonijah, his preemptive behavior as king. As we agreed, Nathan entered and validated my words. David vowed to act that very day. And he did.

The drama of what followed was repeated throughout the palace for months to come. Following prescribed rituals, Priest Zadok and Nathan took the king's donkey on which Solomon rode. Benaiah, David's trusted warrior, gathered servants and assembled the procession for the short journey to Gihon, where Solomon would be anointed king.

I decided to accompany them. With protective soldiers and servants, we made a unique caravan. Benaiah: what a mighty man of valor, friend of Uriah, man of integrity he was. He chose to ride beside me, guided my every step to Gihon. With him at my side, it was as if Uriah's shadow was my protective shade. I had no fear on that chaotic journey. I was filled with God's blessed peace and pride as I saw Solomon, my son, on the throne. King Solomon.

I did not need to learn of my son's consolidation of power from others. He had a throne for me placed beside his. Others might interpret this as a sign of my power. It was not. My throne was a symbol of respect. It became common for people to ask me for favors from the king. I decided to simply present them to Solomon rather than communicate some and not others.

A significant early request came from his older half brother, Adonijah. Smarting from not being anointed king and still plotting to gain the throne for himself, he approached me with a deceptive request.

He asked for Abishag, the beautiful virgin who kept David warm in his bed before his death, to be his wife. Some believed that taking her as his wife would give Adonijah greater claim to the throne. I feared Solomon would take her because of her great beauty. I was equally sure there was no possible way Adonijah could take my son's throne.

So I presented the request.

Seldom did Solomon's mind not follow the same paths as mine. This was an exception.

My Solomon completely misunderstood and made assumptions beyond reason! He implied I would then ask favors to give his father's chief advisors to Adonijah as well. I willed myself to show no emotion at my son's wrong assumptions. It was a matter we would discuss later in private. His public action secured his position as a strong king. He dispatched Benaiah to kill Adonijah for even making such a request.

More blood was spilled. Joab, who had served David nobly, was killed for his allegiance to Adonijah, as were many others.

My heart ached to hear of the bloodshed of those I knew. Most were men who once served well. Each had wives, children. When would this stop? I wished to remove myself from even hearing about the unrest and cleansing as Solomon secured his throne. That was impossible. I was viewed as the queen. I feared becoming a calloused, hardened woman. Abigail assured me that was impossible. She became even wiser as she aged, and I admired her more than ever.

Solomon proved to be wise in ways only God could have granted. His reputation spread to other nations. While his father had focused on wars and subduing others, Solomon's focus was on accumulating wealth.

His trading acumen and willingness to negotiate brought gold, silver, rare timber, copper, horses, chariots, and delicacies beyond description. I shuddered as I saw him compromise God's instructions regarding wives. He acquired women from our greatest foes, idol worshippers and worse. I could not speak of my fears for him regarding this. After all, he had watched his father.

Solomon built quarters for me of grandeur beyond my imagination. He granted my request for Abigail to have quarters next to mine. She fell ill. I stayed at her side and read to her psalms David wrote. I only read the ones of praise and thanksgiving. She slipped peacefully into the arms of death one night. I was there.

Solomon mourned Abigail's passing. He knew of our friendship and how she had guided me through all that life offered. He knew Abigail was my teacher, overseeing the palace in every aspect from its people to what was needed to feed and clothe all. After her death, he wrote an ode to her, "A capable wife." It was recorded thirty-first in a book of proverbs.

Some would say this was written of me. Not so. Only Abigail earned those truthful words.

Many women have done excellently,
    but you surpass them all.
Charm is deceitful, and beauty is vain,

but a woman who fears the Lord is to be praised.
Give her a share in the fruit of her hands,
and let her works praise her in the city gates (Prov. 31:
29-31).

It became my wish that the rest of my life be marked by those words.

STUDY GUIDE
II SAMUEL 11: 1-26, II SAMUEL 12: 24

Bathsheba, like Tamar, has been sadly judged and labeled throughout history. Few think of her as a widow. Many say she was a seducer. She could not have known David was watching her as she performed an expected ritual of bathing. Historians label theirs an affair. Rather it was King David's demand and one-time indulgence in another man's wife. And that man was one of David's most loyal and trusted warriors.

I admire Bathsheba's resilience in circumstances not of her choosing. Her husband murdered, her first son dying, yet she pressed on into her new life. Her story highlights God's immense ability to forgive those who whole-heartedly acknowledge their wrongs and ask His forgiveness. God forgave David and blessed Bathsheba.

In the spring, at the time when kings go off to war,
David sent Joab out with the king's men and the whole
Israelite army. They destroyed the Ammonites and
besieged Rabbah. But David remained in Jerusalem.

One evening David got up from his bed and walked around on the roof of the palace. From the roof he saw a woman bathing. The woman was very beautiful, and David sent someone to find out about her. The man said, "She is Bathsheba, the daughter of Eliam and the wife of Uriah the Hittite." Then David sent messengers to get her. She came to him, and he slept with her. (Now she was purifying herself from her monthly uncleanness.) Then she went back home. The woman conceived and sent word to David, saying, "I am pregnant."

So David sent this word to Joab: "Send me Uriah the Hittite." And Joab sent him to David. When Uriah came to him, David asked him how Joab was, how the soldiers were and how the war was going. Then David said to Uriah, "Go down to your house and wash your feet." So Uriah left the palace, and a gift from the king was sent after him. But Uriah slept at the entrance to the palace with all his master's servants and did not go down to his house.

David was told, "Uriah did not go home." So he asked Uriah, "Haven't you just come from a military campaign? Why didn't you go home?" (II Sam. 11: 1-10)

In the morning David wrote a letter to Joab and sent it with Uriah. In it he wrote, "Put Uriah out in front where the fighting is fiercest. Then withdraw from him so he will be struck down and die."

So while Joab had the city under siege, he put Uriah at a place where he knew the strongest defenders were. When the men of the city came out and fought against Joab, some of the men in David's army fell; moreover, Uriah the Hittite died (II Sam. 11: 14-17).

———

Then David said to Nathan, "I have sinned against the Lord."

Nathan replied, "The Lord has taken away your sin. You are not going to die. But because by doing this you have shown utter contempt for the Lord, the son born to you will die" (II Sam. 12: 13-14).

STUDY QUESTIONS

1. Some have labeled Bathsheba an adulterer. Others state she and David were having an affair. Reading only Scripture, what was Bathsheba's role in the conception of her first child?
2. Why might Bathsheba have become one of David's most influential wives?
3. What position did she have in the life of her son Solomon when he was an adult?
4. How did Bathsheba's life as an older wife show that she was not bound by the traumas of her marriage?

THINKING IT OVER

David's sins, while great, were always forgivable. God is still all-forgiving. Simply agreeing with Him regarding our sin and asking for forgiveness are required.

> …as far as the east is from the west, so far he removes our transgressions from us (Ps. 103: 12).

> …if my people, who are called by my name, will humble themselves and pray and seek my face and turn from their wicked ways, then I will hear from heaven, and I will forgive their sin and will heal their land (II Chron. 7: 14).

> But with you there is forgiveness, so that we can, with reverence, serve you (Ps. 130: 4).

PERSONAL APPLICATION

1. Consider that your past does not define or restrict you in God's eyes.

2. Refuse to let your mind revisit sins God has forgiven. God has forgotten them.

Epilogue

How would we respond if these widows entered our world today? Of course, the details of their lives would be different in our culture, but basic needs are the same. To be accepted in our community, to have their basic needs met: justice, provision, validation of their worth as persons. How would these women be treated in our community, our circle of friends?

Scripture is clear: be compassionate. "Religion that God our Father accepts as pure and faultless is this: to look after orphans and widows in their distress and to keep oneself from being polluted by the world" (James 1: 27). Why be compassionate to the helpless and voiceless? Because God is. God is a father of the fatherless, a defender of widows. In Psalm 68, aliens and prisoners are described as needing compassion. They are often unheard, cannot vote, and are sometimes mistreated.

Being compassionate is being Christ-like. But there's more. Directions about caring for widows and orphans are embedded in Scripture that refer to covenants between God and His people. More than humanitarian aid, though that is sometimes necessary, God instructs that the helpless be comforted, included, and encouraged. Keeping God's covenant is serious business. Yes, covenant-keeping brings blessing. In my experience, serving widows brings great joy.

Whether loving an orphan, adopting children, visiting prisoners, or encouraging widows, compassion flows forward to others and back to satisfy one's own soul.

She is no risk taker who entrusts the very air she breathes moment by moment to her Lord.

CONCLUSION

Romans 12: 2 provides insight for our options: "Do not conform to the pattern of this world, but be transformed by the renewing of your mind. . ."

We can be conformed by our past, restricted by our loss, or we can be transformed and changed. We can be shackled or crushed by our past or remade, remixed, and renewed. To be renewed is to have fresh life of strength or even replacement. That's a world apart from being conformed to who we were before our loss. It's our choice.

Prevail in prayer.

Give in targeted, meaningful ways.

Demonstrate compassion in ways others do not know how to do.

Comfort others with broad experiences of loss.

Live contentedly on less.

Reflect on the characteristics of these widows, and, if you are inclined to journal, write YOUR story.

Acknowledgments

I'm most grateful to Marji Ross, president and publisher of Regnery, for approaching me at NRB in 2016, which resulted in the book you now hold. She not only saw the value of the stories, but encouraged me to pursue their telling in first person narrative.

Thank you Charlie Dyer and Michael Redelynik. I found it impossible to enter the world of each of these widows, to live in their space, smell their bread baking, look through their eyes into the eyes of their husbands. I wanted to walk the path that Naomi and Ruth walked from Moab to Bethlehem. I asked, and all said, "No. Not safe even if you are a seasoned hiker." So I talked with the experts. Charlie and Michael, your willingness and wisdom was so appreciated.

Thank you, Gary Terashita, editor and new friend. With my first ever "first person" writing, your encouragement meant I entered these women's lives more fully. I trust each reader will as well.

Erwin Lutzer, thank you for your affirmation of how I described these amazing women. And reminding me that my husband, Bob, also your friend, would be proud.